Unraveling the Mysteries of Moving to Costa Rica

Unraveling the Mysteries of Moving to Costa Rica
One of the Mainers in Costa Rica series

Published by On The Brink Publishing
7979 NW 21st St.
Doral, FL 33122

ISBN: **978-0-9832065-0-7 [paperback]**
ISBN: **978-0-9832065-1-4 [eBook/PDF]**

Unraveling the Mysteries of Moving to Costa Rica

One of the *Mainers in Costa Rica* Series

Real stories from real people,
what we've learned,
and how it can help you!

Arden Rembert Brink

Table of Contents

Part One · Our Story

Chapter 1—An idea is born   1

Chapter 2—We research the idea 13

Chapter 3—Exploratory trip to Costa Rica 21

Chapter 4—Some factors for success 59

Chapter 5—Moving forward, planning and logistics . . . 77

Chapter 6—Packing and loading the container. 99

Chapter 7—Hannah, the service dog 117

Chapter 8—We've arrived! 127

Part Two · The Ins and Outs of Shipping, Some Practical Advice

Chapter 9—To bring or not to bring 135

Chapter 10—Things we wish we'd brought 147

Chapter 11—Packing it all up 175

Chapter 12—You've loaded the container, now what. . 213

Chapter 13—Other options for shipping 221

Part Three · More Useful Stuff

Research and Resources—A more in-depth look at   233
our research process with suggested resources

How to Choose a Place to Live—Some factors to   253
consider

Budgets—A discussion of expenses, including our   267
original planning budgets, plus real-life current expenses

Reality Check—It's not for everyone; some suggestions 277
for how to determine if it's a good move for *you*

A Few Stories From Folks Who Moved Back—Four   293
first-hand commentaries from folks who move back
to their homeland

Part One

The Mainers Move To
Costa Rica

— Chapter 1

We collapsed gratefully onto the newly made bed. With every towel we owned stuffed around all the leaky windows and doors, we felt that the house was water-*resistant* if not actually water-*tight.* The rain stopped and a mild breeze blew through the open windows, bringing in the low roar of the swollen river just down the hill.

The moon was rising over the mountains out the east-facing bedroom window and the 35-foot triangle of glass making up the west-face of the house seemed alive with the twinkling lights of Puntarenas, twenty miles away. Lightning flashed silently over the ocean beyond.

As we relaxed into sleep, my mind drifted: *yesterday I sure wouldn't have thought we'd be here like this, tonight.*

The day before, we had *attempted* to move in, but had been stopped in our tracks at every turn. Water poured into the house from seemingly every opening. The moving truck got stuck in the unpaved drive and had to be hauled out by a neighbor's backhoe.

The newly connected electrical service was too erratic to run the TV or refrigerator (don't even *think* about the computers!) and we had more than one moment thinking, "ohmigod, what have we done."

But today all was right with the world and we were happily going to bed in our new home, surrounded by all our own belongings, joyfully uncaring that most were still in boxes, the tedious process of unpacking still ahead of us.

I almost didn't want to go to sleep, the views of the moon above and the lights below were so breathtaking. But tiredness overtook before long and sleep settled in. Next thing I knew I was waking to a rosy sunrise out that same east-facing window. I took a few minutes to soak up the beauty of the sunrise before falling asleep again.

This was the Costa Rica we had come for. We'd been here a bit more than a year and a half, and we were in another rental house—not the one we were planning on building someday—but since this house was immediately adjacent to the land we'd bought, that land now served as our "back yard" and we had the view we'd fallen in love with to enjoy every day. Life was good.

For many stories of major life change, it's hard to pinpoint the moment it all began. So much of what we think of as *sudden* change actually happens so gradually that you don't see it until the final explosion—the slow and steady progress in your job "suddenly" results in a huge promotion and a cross-country move, a lifetime intrigue with sailing "suddenly" sees you alone on a sailboat crossing the ocean, the slowly disintegrating marriage "suddenly" ends in divorce. Well, you get the point. Seemingly abrupt changes with gradual and undefined beginnings.

Not so with us. Our change from being normal everyday middle-class residents of the United States to being ex-patriots living in Central America happened in almost exactly one year and began precisely on November 14, 2005 with an article in the *Wall Street Journal.*

More accurately, as long as we're being *precise* here, it began on November 16th when I finally got around to reading the article from the November 14th issue of the *Journal.* (I was perpetually behind in reading the paper, which was an ongoing pet peeve of my husband David's since I also had great difficulty throwing them away without at least a glance at the headlines. So up they piled until the great toppling stack of newspaper made David crazy and I would promise to deal with them.) This issue was near the top of the toppling stack, which was a serendipitous location, very likely increasing the chances of my reading it more thoroughly.

The article in question wasn't really even *about* Costa Rica. That is, it was about the issue of "outsourcing" the baby boomers' retirement. In and of itself I can't say it was all that interesting or why it even caught my attention. But in the course of reading why North Americans are finding places like Costa Rica attractive, an idea was born.

And, as an aside, the article referred—as would have been my tendency until all of this happened—simply to "Americans" meaning people from the United States. Moving to a Central American country has made me far more sensitive to the recognition that Costa Ricans, or Ticos as they're usually called, are obviously "Americans" too, as are the millions of other people living in Central and South America.

Since United Statesians is an awkward term at best, I've at least attempted to add "North" to my use of the term American. Of course, even "North American" is complicated by including Canadians—who *are*

4

flocking to Costa Rica as well—along with Mexicans who are coming in significantly fewer numbers. But there you go. Language is an imperfect thing. Luckily North Americans in Costa Rica are typically referred to as "gringos" and not in a pejorative way, so that pretty much solves the problem. I will use the term gringo a lot; don't be offended.

Back to the idea to move. David has waxed poetic for as long as I've know him about our having a "southern" home in addition to our home in Maine. "Southern" to him did not mean Georgia or Alabama. (Most of the southern United States can't be relied upon in the winter to be consistently warm and the places that can be, such as Florida or Arizona, hold no appeal for us.) Southern to David meant Caribbean. The tropical breeze of a Caribbean island is what he has longed for each year when the long bleak winter settled upon us in Maine.

This idea has surfaced with increasing frequency as the years have passed, he's gotten older, and the chronic nerve pain in his arms has gotten more and more sensitive to cold temperatures. I've always given the idea the attention I felt it deserved, which in my view was *none.*

We basically could not afford our *one* home in Maine. The idea of owning and maintaining a second home was beyond absurd. And David's attachment to the idea wasn't exactly endearing since it was one more case, as far as I was concerned, of his being just a tad disconnected from financial reality.

This background is offered not as husband bashing, but as a bit of useful information to help one understand how *completely* "off-the-wall" it seemed that *I* would suddenly become the proponent of moving to the tropics after squelching David's tropical fantasies for so many years.

(One of my roles in our relationship has always been to be "the money bitch" watching carefully over our expenses, being the damp blanket on many a grand idea. It's an ugly job but somebody's got to do it.)

The epiphany I had reading that *Wall Street Journal* article was that we should not try to have *two* homes, which was clearly impossible. We should simply move to Costa Rica and have *one* home, there.

Now one might wonder why that idea had never occurred to us before. The simple truth is we never knew about Costa Rica before. Oh sure, we'd *heard* of it but that's not saying much. We just never knew of such a place that would offer this magical mixture of characteristics that would be attractive enough to us to relocate there full-time.

(Now, in fairness to David, I should clarify here that *he* says that *he* had been interested in Costa Rica for many years, but since never *once* in the previous twenty years together had the words "Costa Rica" come out of his mouth, I'm gonna stick with my position that "we never knew" about it!)

What are those magical characteristics? Let's start with a simple one, which is also one of the most important to many folks: the weather.

Where in the United States is there mild weather *throughout* the year? Almost nowhere, with the possible exception of some parts of Hawaii, where most of us can't afford to live and perhaps don't even want to. Oh, there might be a few places in California with year-round pleasant weather but, again, California's gotten priced out of the market for most "regular" retirees.

And while those tropical breezes down in the Caribbean islands are balmy and delightful in, say, January, they're just plain hot and nasty in August. I grew up in Louisiana, and David and I moved to Maine from Texas, so we understand *hot*. And we don't want to live in that kind of heat for even half the year. Part of our goal was reducing our cost of living, and having to air-condition your home is not compatible with lowering your expenses. Plus, we just plain don't like it.

Costa Rica's climate is unique in that for a very small country you can find almost any type of weather you want, with the exception of snow. And although we like snow just fine, we've seen enough of it to last us for a long time. Not only had we been in Maine for nearly 20 years but we've both lived in Minnesota in the past, so snow we know. By and large I feel safe in saying we won't miss it. At least, not enough to matter.

Let's see…no snow shoveling, no juggling cars for the snow plowing, no freezing pipes in the winter, no storm windows to be put up every fall, no icy steps to fall down (as had happened before), no icy roads on which to total our car (as had happened before), no blizzards that would trap us in our own home (yes, as had happened before!)… yep, it seemed that we would manage to get by *without* snow.

Okay, Costa Rica doesn't have snow. What *does* it have? While Costa Rica's coasts are both spectacular in their beauty, they are, simply put, hot. Hot and steamy. We immediately eliminated those from our list of prospective places to live. The central valley, on the other hand, offers what is often referred to as "perpetual spring" with temperature (and rainfall) variations based on altitude.

It is a mountainous country and you primarily pick your climate by picking your altitude. We zeroed in on places that claim to offer year round lows in the 60s and highs in the 70s to low 80s, or about 3,000 feet in elevation.

I can remember—at some point in my distant past—thinking that I would miss the change of seasons and would never want to live in a climate where it stayed more or less the same year 'round. I can only say that apparently as the years have gone by I have experienced enough change of seasons that I seem to have had my fill. It just no longer seems to be an issue for me.

And, in fact, Costa Rica *has* seasons—two of them. Usually referred to by Ticos as summer and winter (although just the opposite of our North American summer and winter), they are more accurately thought of as dry (summer) and wet (winter), or "green" as the rainy season is also often called, particularly in the tourist literature.

There's also actually a *third* season you hear less about, which is the "windy season" following on the heels of the rainy season. It's technically part of the "summer" or dry season since the rain has stopped, but the period from late November through roughly January is distinctly windier than the rest of the year. It's the time of year where every Tico you meet will start the conversation with an exaggerated shiver and the words "muy frio" (very cold). They break out the furry lined boots and winter jackets, yet welcome it because it means two things: the rain has ended and Christmas is coming!

But, back to the two *primary* seasons—even the wet season isn't wet all the time. Generally speaking—at least in the central valley of which most everything I say is referring—this is not the torrential-rains-for-days-on-end that we think of when we hear the term "rainy season." More typically the day dawns bright and sunny, it clouds over and rains in the afternoon, and clears off again for a starlit evening with the brutal exception of September and/or October when it can, indeed, rain off and on all day for days on end.

So while climate is in many ways only a backdrop to the rest of life, it was an important underlying factor in both why we'd never seriously considered moving anywhere else full time and why we were suddenly considering Costa Rica. And looking back at that *Wall Street Journal* article, it certainly didn't focus on the climate. Or, for that matter, the lower cost of living or the warmth and friendliness of the people or any of the rest of the reasons that we came to think of Costa Rica as our new home. But it planted a seed, somehow, that was beginning to take root and grow almost immediately.

In truth, as I reflect upon this point of "the beginning" of the idea to move to Costa Rica, I'm compelled to add another slightly more peculiar note.

Longer ago than November 2005, somewhere perhaps even a year before that, I woke up one morning from a vivid dream about *buying land in Costa Rica.* The actual plot of the dream is long gone in my memory, but here's what I do remember: Later that morning I watched as all my email trickled in from overnight while my computer had been off and one of the emails beckoned in big, glorious color "Buy Land in Costa Rica."

I was stunned.

I'm a *very* rational and logical person and it seemed unlikely to me that I had truly *dreamt* that I was going to receive this email. So I conjectured to myself that another similar email had probably arrived sometime in the past and while I hadn't taken conscious note of it, I must have processed it at some deeper level, hence the dream.

And now, it was pure coincidence that the email had popped up again on this very day after the dream. I deleted the email and really didn't give it much further thought. It wasn't until months into our process that I remembered the dream and the email advertisement.

So, who knows? Maybe *that* was actually the beginning of the idea.

—Chapter 2

Was I nuts? Since the idea seemed a bit crazy, even to me—and it was *my* idea!—I realized I'd best do some preliminary research before I dared mention it to anyone. Thank God for the internet. Even in 2005 there was lots of information online and today, of course, there's so much more.

Initial searches in Google turned up thousands of websites, a few of which provided lots of good detailed information. (I've since come to learn that much of it is actually incorrect, though, so keep a little healthy skepticism about you as you do your research.)

At least the fundamentals of what I'd gleaned from the *Wall Street Journal* article were confirmed. The central valley really did have weather that justified the description of "year 'round spring," the medical care and education *did* seem remarkably advanced for a so-called third world nation, and the cost of living looked to be substantially less than a comparable quality of life anywhere in the U.S. that we would consider living.

(A note on Costa Rica's "third world" status: it is now generally referred to as an under-developed

13

country, or more optimistically a "developing nation" rather than third world. And I'd have to say that change seems appropriate to its actual state of development. At the same time, the difference is hardly worth quibbling over. It quite clearly is *not* the U.S. This is an important distinction since many folks make the mistake of thinking they're moving to a less-expensive U.S. and despite the availability of McDonald's, Walmart, T.G.I.Fridays and U.S. network television, it is indisputably not the United States. Not fully "grokking" this fact is going to set you up for misery.)

So after a few days of stealthy research I felt like I knew enough to float the idea past the family. That evening, as a chill wind was cutting through the poorly weather-stripped windows of our 200 year old house, we gathered around the fireplace with our cocktails and I gently broached the idea, prepared to just let it go if either David or my octogenarian parents thought I was nuts. But as I explained what I'd found out thus far in my initial research, they all agreed—enthusiastically!—that they liked the idea.

Okay!

Amazingly enough, we were on our way.

For the next six months, life went along as usual on the surface—I went to work everyday, continued on with my Buddhist classes, took care of Mom and Dad, and battled a long, snowy Maine winter.

Beneath the surface, of course, *everything* felt the opposite of "as usual." I knew I couldn't say anything at work yet since I would need—financially—to work right up until our departure and was concerned that the company wouldn't be amenable to that once they knew.

So under a façade of "business as usual" was a swirl of activity. (In "Part Three, More Useful Stuff," I've given a much more detailed look at the resources we used, and some new ones that I can suggest.)

I prowled our local bookstores, buying whatever I could find about *living* in Costa Rica, while completely ignoring the travel guides. We'd never been to Costa Rica, but we figured if we moved there we'd have plenty of time to travel and see the sights.

I didn't need to know about beachfront hotels. I needed to know how much it cost to build a house and what we would have to pay for groceries. I became a master at snooping around the internet.

I discovered the world of online forums where I could essentially eavesdrop on conversations of others who were either already living in Costa Rica or, like me, researching the idea. There's a lot of good information to be found in all of the forums, although like all things internet, it's wise to keep that virtual salt-shaker handy and take the advice with the proverbial grain of salt.

Nothing we read dissuaded us from the idea, although we did keep our eyes open for the deal breaker. As time went on and we didn't find one, we began to be more and more committed to the plan, which resulted in our being less and less interested in unearthing problems. As our emotional investment grew, I found I didn't even want to *read* anything negative. I think I was afraid that I might actually *find* that deal breaker, and I didn't want the deal to be broken!

In fact, I began to take it "personally" when I would hear about people who had moved to Costa Rica and then moved back to the states. I felt strangely betrayed, as though they (all people who did not know me, at *all*, nor I them other than through reading their words) were "giving up" in defeat. It was an admittedly strange reaction on my part, one that I could look at rationally and recognize as crazy, but I nonetheless *felt* the betrayal. It was as though their returning to the U.S. somehow invalidated our burgeoning plans to move *to* Costa Rica.

At the time of our research, I desperately wanted to get some insights from what I came to think of as "real people" and searched (mostly in vain) for first-person accounts. One of the few I found was written by Martin Rice, and although I didn't find the book to be all I'd hoped—it was essentially a compilation of letters which always seems like a fast and easy way to write a book, but (in *my* view) produces a book that simply isn't very engaging—it was, still, a first person account and for that I enjoyed it.

For whatever literary flaws I found, I felt like Martin and Robin were relatively "real people" who had moved to Costa Rica and I was actually stunned when I discovered his blog and found that they were in the process—literally *while* I was reading his book—of moving back to the states. I actually wrote him from the "contact" link on his website to ask (in a very roundabout and subtle way) "why?"

Although I wouldn't have blamed him for ignoring me, or perhaps replying that he owed me no explanation, he wrote back a nice response that simply said there was no secret "behind the scenes" reasoning, but merely that he wanted to ensure Robin's security in the future and this seemed better done in the states.

I talk more in Chapter 4 about the "factors for success" and what are some of the things that keep people here vs. send them back to their homeland, so I bring it up at this point primarily as an observation about the depth to which we were becoming committed to the plan. Anything that might "mess with" the plan came as unwelcome input.

Frankly, of course, at this early stage it truly was more of an "idea" than a "plan" despite my sometimes using the terms interchangeably. Our efforts to make a true "plan" were surely hindered somewhat by the simple fact that we'd never set foot in Costa Rica before. Having an "idea" to move there was intriguing and a bit daring. Having a "plan" to move there was perhaps simply lunacy!

We knew we needed to get our feet on the ground at least once before doing anything irrevocable, so we began to make a plan for a reconnaissance visit. By February, about 3 months after the birth of the idea, I had made internet "friends" with Jeanetta Owens of Las Terrazas B&B in Grecia. Jeanetta was relentlessly kind in taking time to answer my emails and offer her insights and advice.

From all that we'd read, we knew Grecia was one of the towns that interested us, so the combination of Jeanetta's geographic location and her natural proclivity for helpfulness led us to form a plan to fly to Costa Rica, stay at the B&B she and her husband, Charles, owned and see what we found.

Just as with our criteria for book selection, we had no interest this trip in tourist attractions, but wanted to see where we would want to live, or as some would point out, *if* we even wanted to live there. We had looked before at the tours available and had come to the conclusion that they were expensive so were just going to sort it out on our own.

My parents needed to have some assistance around the clock—Daddy, with his Parkinson's, was somewhat prone to falling, unfortunately more than once taking Mom down with him by accident, so we'd found that we were reluctant to leave them on their own. And certainly for us to be away for any period of time, there was no question but that my brother, presumably with his family, would need to come to Maine to stay with them. Although this first came up in February (more on *that* later!) it was to be July before it could actually be put together.

So, the months went by, we continued our research, and continued to firm up our commitment—to ourselves, at least—to make this radical life move.

Still without ever having spent one moment actually *in* Costa Rica.

— Chapter 3

Finally it was coming together: my brother, Hans, and his family found a time that could work for them to leave Philadelphia and come stay for a while in Maine so that we could go to Costa Rica. They would come for the last 10 days or so of July and early part of August. Part of the time would be just my brother and his young daughter and part of the time his wife, MaryPat, would join them.

Just as our dates began to shape up, I read a glowing recommendation on Costa Rica Living (the Yahoo group) about George Lundquist's tour, Retire On Social Security, and we took a second look. As I describe in Part Three, "More Useful Stuff," we'd formed the opinion that the tours were expensive and that with the generous help of people like Jeanetta we could do it on our own.

But the perfect "match-up" of George's once-monthly tour and our travel dates seemed almost like destiny, and after reading the various testimonials on George's own site and the online discussion groups, we decided to take the plunge and sign up.

From our reading, we'd already decided that the beaches were out—too much heat and humidity for us—and we'd grown used to country living in Maine, so the city of San Jose and immediate surrounding areas seemed of little interest. As I mentioned before, Grecia—from all we read—seemed like the sort of place we might like. We also included Heredia on our initial list, again just based on our reading and the fact that it was a "college town" which fit our ideas of the right place for us. We later got enough sense that Heredia was too "dense" for us, too big of a city, and ruled it out—a decision that was completely reinforced the first time we actually traveled into the city, a city that to this day we dislike and avoid whenever possible!

As we read about Grecia, we would repeatedly read references to San Ramon as offering a similar climate and environment so we added that to the mental list of possibilities, and Puriscal came to our consciousness somewhere along the way, too, and was added.

Finally, I'd struck up an email conversation with a fellow in the Orosi valley who spoke of it glowingly, so we thought that might be an option to consider. The fact that these were *all* the places George included on his tour again seemed like fate, solidifying our faith that we'd made the right choice.

Trying to make the trip on the tightest budget possible, we searched for a decent airfare. We finally settled on a slightly hellish itinerary that took us from Portland, Maine, through New York and Atlanta before finally heading on to San Jose, with 4+ hour layovers in both airports. But the fare was right, and we figured for this trip we had more time than money.

We had hoped to fly on the 22nd of July, leaving us free to celebrate my dad's and Hans' birthdays on the 21st, but we felt that the risk of something going wrong in our travels, possibly causing us not to arrive until the following day—thus missing the beginning of the tour—was just too scary so we reluctantly opted to forego the birthday celebrations and fly on the 21st.

Luckily, all three legs of the flight went smoothly and we arrived in San Jose airport on the night of the 21st. The Hotel Villa Bonita where we were staying had said they'd send a driver, but the chaotic scene that met us when we emerged from immigration and customs was almost overwhelming and we never did see anyone who appeared to be waiting for us.

We finally opted for a cab (having cleverly printed out the directions from the internet just for such a potential situation) and found ourselves at the hotel in mere minutes. (Turns out that the hotel had, indeed, sent a driver whom they now had to call and relieve from duty; we were apologetic but sure felt like we'd looked pretty thoroughly so didn't exactly feel like it was our fault.)

We were shown our room and were happy to settle down to sleep since it had been a long day of travel, and coming from the east coast of the U.S. our bodies thought it was two hours later than the clock showed. (Costa Rica is in the Central time zone, but doesn't go to Daylight Savings Time the way the majority of the U.S. does, so during the seven or eight months of Daylight Savings Time, for all practical purposes Costa Rica "slides over" into Mountain time, resulting in a two hour time difference for us.) No air conditioning in the hotel, but with the ceiling fan we were comfortable and slept well.

Morning brought what seemed to us to be an amazing discovery—there were no screens in the windows! I'd grown up in the south where mosquitoes were very common, and in Maine the slightest crack in your screen door or rip in a window screen was an invitation to seemingly thousands of buzzing, biting mosquitoes, so this seemed truly astounding. I kept popping my arm out through the open jalousie windows like some sort of demented jack-in-the-box, simply marveling at that even being *possible.*

This marked one of our first "favorite things" about Costa Rica—there really are very few mosquitoes, at least in the central valley. (Even in the "buggiest" areas we've visited on the coasts and in the "jungles" we've never experienced the thick swarms of mosquitoes that we'd lived with for years in Maine, and even now after several years in San Ramon, I can count on one hand the mosquitoes we've seen.)

After I'd sufficiently amazed myself sticking my arm out the screen-free window (okay, I'm easily amused!) we emerged for the breakfast that was included in our room rate. We ate on a lovely back porch and finally experienced the famed Costa Rican *gallo pinto*. This rice and black-bean dish is ubiquitous throughout the country (we've heard tell that on the Caribbean side they make a variation that has coconut milk in it, but virtually everywhere else in the country it's white rice, black beans, possibly some bit of sautéed onion and peppers, seasoned with the local Lizano salsa) and everything I'd read told of how the Ticos ate gallo pinto for breakfast which I'd had a hard time imagining.

I mean, we actually were quite fond of rice and beans, and one of my classic Maine side dishes was a "Cuban-esque" yellow rice mixed right at the end with black beans, so it's not as though the flavor concept was foreign to us. It was the "breakfast" thing that seemed strange. Rice and beans for breakfast?

Well, turns out I liked it just fine and to this day am perfectly happy with gallo pinto for breakfast.

25

David, not so much, although in a pinch he'll eat it. (He's a natural fan of sweet food for breakfast, though, and I'm the kind that's happy with a cheeseburger for breakfast, so you can see how that goes.) Although *Thirty Days of Food*, another book in this series, is full of recipes for all sorts of food, gallo pinto is such a *definitive* classic that I'm going to tell you right here how to make it. That way even if you never come to Costa Rica, you can get up in the morning and pretend you're here:

Gallo Pinto

1 /2 to 1 onion
1 /4 to 1 /2 sweet red (bell) pepper
chopped garlic, optional
cooked rice
cooked black beans
olive oil
salt and pepper to taste
Lizano salsa
chopped cilantro, optional

Dice (chop into fairly small pieces) the onion and bell pepper. Heat a skillet with a good splash of olive oil and sauté the onion and pepper for a few minutes. If you like, add a clove of garlic, chopped, or a small spoonful of chopped garlic from the jar. Even though it's breakfast, a small amount of garlic will add to the flavor of the dish without seeming overwhelming.

Add about 1 cupful of cooked white rice (cooked brown rice can be used, and will certainly make a healthier gallo pinto, but it won't produce the classic flavor or texture) and a cupful of cooked drained black beans. (You can cook these yourself in your crock-pot or just use canned which are fine!) Stir the whole business around in the skillet until heated through. Add a good splash of Lizano sauce and stir in chopped cilantro to taste.

A typical Tico breakfast or lunch might well consist of *just* the gallo pinto, although adding fried or scrambled eggs alongside is also perfectly acceptable and rounds it out to a tastier breakfast, in my view.

Lizano is actually a brand name and they make a number of different salsas and condiments, but when people just say "Lizano" they mean their basic, standard sauce which is unique to Costa Rica. Not at all spicy—nothing, in fact, like we gringos think of when we hear the word "salsa"—it's probably closer to Worcestershire sauce than anything else, and even that isn't a great comparison. It can be bought now in the U.S. online and in a few specialty stores, and is surely a favorite item for travelers to put in their suitcases after a visit to Costa Rica.

After a leisurely breakfast we got directions about which way was which, and headed out into Alajuela for our first real look at Costa Rica. We found a Mas x Menos (said as "mas por menos" or "more for less") grocery store and were surprised to see the tellers and managers wearing "Walmart" name tags. (Walmart, we were to find out, had recently bought a good-sized stake in a number of local grocery chains, as well as having bought completely the Hipermas chain which is now, essentially, a regular Walmart albeit with a somewhat different product mix, presumably to better serve the local market.)

27

I also discovered that the sandals I had brought were rubbing my foot (which was strange since they were shoes I'd been wearing all summer, go figure) so we found a Pay-Less shoe store, of all things, and managed to transact our first purchase in Spanish. Muddled, pigeon Spanish, to be sure, but since it produced the desired result, we felt a surge of exultation—maybe we *would* be able to manage in this Spanish-speaking country after all!

The tour began bright and early the next morning, meeting up with George Lundquist himself and the other three couples on the tour. George is a brash, loud-spoken former Texan who, we learned right away, has opinions—strong ones—and voices them freely. It is, in his view, what you're paying him for.

But we would learn that he also does an excellent job of having you understand this is "his opinion" he's expressing, his experiences and stories he's telling, and his job is to give you enough information to be able to make up your *own* mind about things.

At this point, though, we really knew none of this yet. We just knew we'd signed on to spend the next three and a half days in a small bus with these three other couples, George, and his Tico driver, Oscar. After a relatively brief introductory session, we loaded 'em up and headed out.

We hit Grecia first, which had been on our "short list" almost from the beginning. As we piled out of the little bus and walked through the town park to the little "bandstand" or pavilion in the center, we listened to George talk about Grecia itself, but even more about small towns in general in Costa Rica. While I promptly forgot everything specific he said, I know David and I both had a feeling of reassurance that this introduction to the country was going to be useful and was going to reinforce our intentions to move here. We just plain liked it.

(Speaking of reassurance, I'm going to offer a bit right here to anyone who is reading this and considering taking George's tour: I speak often of the "little bus" because when *we* took the tour, in 2006, George indeed had a *little* bus. It was the kind of bus that required an odd folding seat configuration to get everyone in, leaving some people sitting in skimpy jump-seats and others piled three across in a not-all-that-big (or comfortable) bench seat. Since we had no expectations otherwise, it served us just fine. And, in fact, the "little-ness" of the bus seemed to be a part of the whole experience. George had already made plans to buy a much larger bus, with an actual center aisle and more standard "bus" seating and I think we were one of the last tours before he took possession of his new beauty. So don't be alarmed by any "little bus"

29

references I make! While I actually remember the little bus rather fondly, most people are more than happy to realize that the "new" bus is much more commodious.)

After walking around Grecia a bit, stopping into an appliance store to get a feel for what's available, we piled back into the bus and headed further up the hill. Somewhere during the day we went to Sarchi, a small town famed throughout Costa Rica for its furniture manufacturing, and ate lunch at a local restaurant with striking views out over the valleys, aptly named La Mirador (Spanish for overlook or viewpoint). I ate what was to be my first plate, of many over the next 10 days, of arroz con camarones (rice with shrimp) which is essentially like an oriental "shrimp fried rice" without the soy sauce. Still one of my favorites.

As the afternoon wound down, we drove through San Ramon and ended up at La Posada, a very pleasant hotel on the north side of town. Throughout the tour George handled actual "check-in" for hotels, meal tabs, and other logistics of travel so it was completely easy. We simply went where we were told.

In this case we went into our assigned bedroom and found the most amazing bed. A quick check with our tour-mates revealed that while they were all different, they were all spectacular in various ways. Okay, I guess every hotel has to be "known" for something and the beds are definitely note-worthy at La

Posada! All made of brightly varnished hardwoods, they ranged from our deranged antlers to more traditional but equally impressive head-and-footboard arrangements.

The bed in our first room at La Posada. You had to watch your eyes a bit to be sure you didn't poke one out on the antler-like headboard...

After ooh-ing and ahh-ing at all the strange beds, we settled down in the courtyard for a beer and some conversation about what we'd seen so far, followed by dinner at Mi Choza (alternately spelled Mi Chosa, depending on whether you believe their sign or their menu!), a local San Ramon favorite. George introduced us to chicharrones, a Tico specialty of deep fried pork chunks that vary from almost inedible to quite yummy, depending on where you eat them. George accurately advised that Mi Choza made very good ones.

After dinner a group of the guests walked to Pops ice cream shop while some of us (me, included, with my hip arthritis as my excuse) were happy to ride over with Oscar in the little bus. Everyone made their ice cream selection and we stood around and ate, while George admitted that the ice cream cost more than the dinner had!

He wasn't complaining—just recognizing the difference between typical Tico restaurant prices and the admittedly high ice cream prices. It's a good lesson in general—if you want to spend less money eating out in Costa Rica, don't go to the U.S. "imports" or even the Costa Rica "chains" since they'll almost always cost more than a true local business.

We gratefully settled down into our antlers-gone-wild bed, hours earlier than we would have considered normal for bedtime, but tired from a long, full day. As we settled in with our books, though, we realized the lighting was pretty grim for reading, a phenomenon that was to be repeated at practically every other hotel we've ever stayed at in Costa Rica (and Nicaragua, for that matter).

It has taken us years of living here to fully grasp—at the risk of making generalizations—that they just aren't "readers" here. While there are probably (sadly) some more profound ramifications of that, one of the most visible is simply that they don't use lamps. It's rare to find a room illuminated by anything other than the ceiling light fixture and even the tourist industry doesn't seem to recognize the typical gringo's need for bedside illumination. Ah well.

Breakfast the following morning was very good— more gallo pinto for me, with *huevos revueltos* or scrambled eggs and *salchicha* which might translate as sausage but was, in fact, a hot dog! It was all served in a very nicely appointed hotel dining room (which seemed to be a bit underutilized, only serving breakfast, but then they didn't ask my advice!) and we met Jim and Ben, two "Americanos" who had a number of lots for sale around the San Ramon area.

We had two astounding revelations as we spent the morning with them looking at land. First, we realized that you could not only have land here with gorgeous mountain and valley views, but also with *water* views of the Gulf of Nicoya and even, at times, the open Pacific Ocean! Ohmigod, that was something we hadn't counted on and really changed our whole idea of what we thought we might be looking for in a place to live.

Second, we visited site after site where the wind simply *howled*, where it was truly hard to stand up in the face of the fierce breeze, often on bare hillsides where the view was fantastic as long as you looked way beyond to the ocean, but pretty bleak once you brought your view back down to earth and looked at your immediate surroundings. You didn't have to be much of a visionary to look around and realize that this vast expanse of rolling green hillside was going to be an entirely different place in a few years when each of those "ready-to-build" *planteles*, or house-sites would be covered with a house.

We were spoiled after twenty years in Maine with our eighteen acres and only one house in sight (albeit an unfortunate architectural monstrosity) and the idea of these tree-less hillsides dotted with houses was unappealing to us. No worries. As George would keep telling us, a major goal of the tour was to help us identify what we wanted *and* what we didn't want.

Another key thing that happened on that Monday in San Ramon was a conversation we had with Ben about cost of living. From all that we'd been reading, we'd developed the idea that we hoped to spend $500 a month for rent which would fit our budget and *seemed* like a viable amount. But like almost everything we'd done so far, we'd gotten this idea from *reading* and not from actually talking with any real people currently living here.

So on one of those windblown vibrant green hillsides, we had a moment to talk with Ben and test our theory. Could we really rent a good-sized house here for $500 a month? Bear in mind that we were two full families in one household—David and me *plus* my parents—with dogs, cats, a grand piano, Daddy's painting studio, and lots of "stuff" so we weren't talking about renting an efficiency apartment. We didn't need fancy, but we needed some space, and it had to be *reasonably* livable by our admittedly *soft* North American standards.

Imagine our delight when Ben replied that not only was $500 an *adequate* budget for rent in this area, he thought we would be hard-pressed to spend more than $350 or so! *(It's important to note that this was in 2006 and these figures are no longer applicable. Be sure to read the "Budgets" section in Part Three, More Useful Stuff!)*

Even though we hadn't made a decision yet that San Ramon was "it"—especially since George hammers on *not* making any decisions until you've finished the whole tour!—we were elated with this confirmation of the validity of our planning thus far.

Two more pieces began to fall into place on this San Ramon morning, making it a very productive five hours. After looking at various house-sites—the idea being *not* to sell us any, but to show us examples of what was available and how much to expect to pay for it—Oscar, our trusty Tico driver, turned off the "pista" (the main highway) and powered the little bus up a remarkably steep and alarmingly narrow road.

At the top was a clearing with three small cabinas under construction, which turned out to be a new project of Ben's. The cabinas were rustic and modestly-sized, but well laid out so that they would have two bedrooms, decent bath, small but functioning kitchen with eat-in area, and living room. Ben said they were due to be finished in the next couple of months and would be for rent, fully-furnished with all utilities, ready to move into.

Again, stressing to ourselves that we hadn't actually *decided* anything yet, this provided another missing piece of the puzzle, which was *how* and *where* to actually *land* once we got here. When you're just "regular folks" you simply get on a plane, land here, stay at a hotel, and sort things out. Or at least that's how it seemed to us since we were anything *other* than regular folks.

This is long before we knew we'd be arriving with nineteen suitcases (more on that *later!*) but even just imagining landing with Mom and Dad and the critters was enough to give pause. So at least here was the kernel of a plan forming, a place we could imagine coming to stay while we waited for our container and moving into our regular rental house. Add one more point for San Ramon.

The last piece that was reassuring to us was our trip to the Plaza Occidente, more commonly known (at least among the gringos) as "the mall" conveniently situated at the entrance to San Ramon. While the mall

36

itself, once we lived here, has proven to be only minimally interesting, what we saw on this vital day of the tour was encouraging.

What we found was a pharmacy with a delightful woman pharmacist who spoke some English; a supermarket that didn't look *all* that different from the grocery stores we knew back home (admittedly a bit smaller, but very clean, modern, bright, and well-stocked with completely recognizable food and packaged goods); a GNC (General Nutrition Center) store full of the familiar U.S. branded supplements; a 3-screen movie theater showing current releases (typically in English, with Spanish sub-titles); and a food court with Burger King, Kentucky Fried Chicken, Church's Chicken, and Papa John's Pizza. It was one more confirmation that life here would be different, but not completely outside the realm of the familiar.

We finally left the mall, piling back into our little bus, feeling entirely encouraged about our plans to move to Costa Rica. The next stop at the viveros (plant nurseries) in La Garita answered questions we didn't even realize we'd had—will we be able to afford to garden and landscape our home in Costa Rica? Well, our stop at just one of the *many* viveros in La Garita was easily enough to answer *that* question. Yes. Yes, yes, and yes. Plants here are not only spectacularly lush, but cheap. Just plain cheap. Woo-hoo!

Citrus trees, about a meter tall (39"), sold for about $2. Same for avocados, palms, and mangos. Bougainvillea plants in every imaginable color stretched seemingly for miles, each robust blooming plant selling for about $1.50, with much bigger ones going for just under $3. It was mind-boggling, just seeing how much "plant" you could get for your money.

We had never been much for gardening, although I tended to fantasize about it over the years. Part of the reason my green-thumb tendencies stayed latent, living primarily in fantasyland, was simply economic—plants are *expensive* in the U.S.

I can still remember vividly when we bought our home in Maine—we'd been renting for years and now finally *owned* the land around us which inspired a new-found passion for gardening catalogs. Like people throughout the northern climes, I spent hours poring over the colorful catalogs during the cold winter months and placed a good-sized order, eagerly awaiting the arrival at the proper time (months later) for planting according to our location.

Finally, the long-awaited delivery arrived and I was stunned—and *not* in a good way!—to realize that those lovely photos of the plants I'd ordered showed *mature* plants, and that what I had actually purchased were *twigs*, two to four inches tall, that I was supposed to plant and apparently wait a *very* long time for them to grow up.

Although it's true that delayed gratification has some benefits—and I was, indeed, genuinely delighted when my peonies finally bloomed years later—the fact that those tiny twigs were virtually the only kinds of plants I could afford in Maine, coupled with financial inaccessibility of hired help for the heavier labor, made gardening stay primarily in the *back* of my mind.

Here we were seeing a solution to both of those issues and visions of lush tropical gardens suddenly bloomed forth as yet one more reason to put on our "yes, let's move to Costa Rica" list.

There were other stops along the way that day, and we wrapped up another very busy day in Puriscal. Our B&B stay for that night was a simple one, but with adequate accommodations and our first introduction to the so-called "suicide shower" which we've come to learn is universally used by Ticos (if they have hot water at all) and is *very* likely to be present in your shower should you rent a Tico house when you move here.

Truthfully, I think the dangers from a suicide shower are probably no greater, and perhaps even smaller, than the often over-looked risk of slipping and falling in the bathtub or your standard north American shower, but there *is* something admittedly unnerving about mixing electricity and water in quite such close proximity, especially when you consider Ticos tend to have bad wiring in general.

A suicide shower, for those who aren't familiar with this local gem, is a fixture that features an electrical water heating system right in the showerhead. There is one faucet (not counting the "bathtub" type spout or plain old outdoor spigot that will typically be found down low, about a foot off the ground on the shower wall) and when you turn on the water, it flows past this heating element before sprinkling out of the little holes onto your head.

It's actually a wildly efficient unit, heating only as much water as you need, and supplying it endlessly should you be inclined to take long showers. It also encourages water conservation (notwithstanding the part I just said about long showers) because the water temperature is directly (and inversely) proportional to the volume of water flowing. So, the higher the water pressure (i.e. usage) the cooler the water.

Or, perhaps said the more meaningful way, the lower the water pressure, the warmer the shower. A well-functioning suicide showerhead allows for an adequate shower at a pleasantly hot temperature, but emphasis should be on the "adequate" with no illusions of a forceful flow.

As far as safety goes, there's always someone somewhere who will trot out a horror story of someone they knew (or maybe someone that they knew, knew, in the classic form of urban legends) who was electrocuted by their suicide shower, but again I venture to say that they are no more deadly than the actual act of bathing is, in general, when you consider the very real risk of simply slipping and falling in the shower. On the other hand, I will also say that common sense suggests that you keep your wet hands away from the fixture itself! After all, let's not be silly here. Wet hands and electrical wires just seem like a bad combination.

We successfully navigated our first suicide shower without incident so felt we'd passed another test in our readiness to live in Costa Rica. Thus began another day of the tour. We got a chance to see more of Puriscal on this morning, and we both found that it didn't, shall we say, *speak* to us as a place we wanted to live, at least not as loudly as San Ramon had. But we didn't completely rule it out either, and planned to return after the tour to look further.

The rest of the day was interesting, but uneventful, culminating in our stay at Pico Blanco, which was one of the most peculiar hotels I'd even been in. *(Small note, they don't stay there on the tour anymore.)* High up in the Escazú hills, it was selected primarily for its spectacular valley views at night, and for that it was indeed worthwhile. There, in fact, was nothing *wrong* with the place, it was just eerily empty.

41

It was a large complex, with lavish marble floors and sweeping staircases, corridors and arches…the entire impression was much more fitting a European haunted castle that a modestly priced Costa Rican hotel, but the strangest of all was simply that we had the impression that we were the only people there, amongst all this grandeur and immense size.

Two eventful things happened during our strange Pico Blanco stay. One was that we met Barry Wilson of Ship Costa Rica on that final morning of the tour. George told the tale of his own disastrous experience moving a fairly small amount of his household and personal goods when he had moved here, and how as a result he spent the first years of his tour advising people it was better just to sell it all, give it to the kids, leave it behind, and replace things here.

Then, he'd met Barry through some of his former tour clients and now neighbors who had used him to ship their container and been exceptionally pleased, especially in contrast to George's experience. So now George recommended Barry and introduced him to us at breakfast.

As we sat at the breakfast table, Barry said a few words in his mellow, still slightly Canadian-accented voice and opened it up to questions. Unfortunately, none of us even knew what questions to ask, so the actual presentation wasn't terribly helpful in the sense of any information imparted. But it was hugely helpful in one key way—now we felt that we had a resource, that we were no longer flailing around in the dark when it came to the whole issue of shipping. Under pressure from all of us on the tour, he also had tossed out some very ballpark prices and the six to eight thousand dollars for a container that he mentioned (remember this was in 2006) was *immensely* more appealing than the $26,000 quotes that we'd gotten thus far. *(Much more on these quotes later, but just to be clear here, the $26,000 was for two containers, but even doubling Barry's ballpark gave us a much better figure than what we had.)*

The second notable experience we had at Pico Blanco was that David tripped on the last step as he came down the grand staircase on his way to breakfast, crashing to his knee on the unforgiving marble floor. It hurt like hell, and dripped blood rather unappealingly down his leg throughout breakfast, but what was to become much more impactful was that it ultimately swelled up and made it very difficult for him to drive, walk, or get around. Stay tuned... this will matter to us later.

After our breakfast with Barry, we piled into our little bus for the final day of the tour and headed through San Jose to the east side and our visit to Cartago and the Orosi valley. We all liked the look of

Cartago—it felt a bit more "European" and less "third world"—and there is no question that the Orosi valley is beautiful. Truly spectacular.

For us, though, one huge problem seemed to eliminate it from our list of prospective places to live, and that was simply its location being on the *east* side of San Jose, which meant to go to the Pacific beaches or, even more critically perhaps, to go to the airport to pick up visiting friends and family, to go *anywhere* really, meant traveling *through* the city of San Jose. Yuck.

I know there are folks who drive in San Jose all the time, and I'm sure there are some who see our distaste for it as silly. But our impressions driving through the city, even safely ensconced in the bus, not having to *do* the actual driving, was still a harrowing experience and there's no way around it. It's ugly, it's difficult to get around with an assortment of strange (unmarked, of course) turns, it has a slightly "dangerous" feel as most inner cities tend to, and it made for a long drive to and from the airport.

We had already discovered that my brother and his family were vehemently opposed to this move (more on *that* later, too) and I knew that the first time we picked them up at the airport and made this long, ugly trek through the city to get home, it wouldn't matter how lovely the Orosi valley was. They were going to pack Mom and Dad up in their suitcases if they had to and take them back to the U.S. with them.

David, too, now having gotten a taste for having a home where we not only had beautiful mountain views but *ocean views* as well, was not interested in giving that up. So, for many reasons, the Orosi area was stricken from our list, and we've never been sorry. It *is* beautiful, though, so for folks with different needs than ours, it has much to recommend it. (Be aware, though, by almost all accounts, it does get more rain than many other areas which has the advantage of keeping it greener, so may or may not be seen as a negative. To each their own....)

On that final Wednesday afternoon of the tour we returned to San Jose and the group dispersed. Although we were still planning on returning to each of the three major areas—San Ramon, Puriscal, and even Orosi—in the coming week to hopefully settle for good the question of where we wanted to live, we had to *start* somewhere, and we'd made a plan to meet Ben the following day in San Ramon. Now all we had to do was get from San Jose to San Ramon.

Our minimal Spanish skills didn't seem sufficient to negotiate a decent cab fare, so George kindly stepped in to assist. All the rates seemed too high to him, so he conferred briefly with Oscar and they offered to have us just stay on the bus and Oscar would take us to San

Ramon for a flat $50. We were a little daunted by having to leave the safe cocoon of George's tour and strike out on our own, so extending to the last possible moment our time in the security of known hands was wonderful. So, off we went, checking into La Posada about an hour later.

The next morning Ben met us bright and early—remember this was in late July, thus in the middle of the rainy season, so doing anything outdoors required an early start if you wanted to miss the rain—and we headed off to look at land. We took George's advice—and everything else we'd ever read—seriously and had no intentions of actually *buying* land on this trip. We just wanted to hopefully settle on where we thought we *would eventually* buy land so that when we moved in a few months we could rent in the same area where we would be building.

One reason for this was the somewhat obvious one of being near the eventual construction so that we could properly oversee building. The other, though, was a little more subtle of a reason but equally important, which is simply that we wanted to begin building *our life,* not just our home. So we wanted to start off our new life right when we got here, not just be biding our time by renting somewhere other than where we planned eventually to settle.

By now David's injured knee was really bothering him, and he stretched out across the backseat of Ben's new Land Rover, groaning occasionally as we bumped over back-roads. We described to Ben the situation that we had in Maine which was "acreage" that had come with a house where we lived, and that had sufficient land for us to subdivide and sell off four house lots. The revenue from the lot sales would, in theory, pay off our house. (Since all our property ended up going on sale just as the housing market crashed in the U.S., there's a heavy emphasis on the "in theory" part of that statement, but at that time we were blissfully unaware of what was to come.)

We initially hoped to do something similar in Costa Rica, although in the past months as we'd formulated a plan for our move, we'd also been going through hell trying to get our simple four-lot "subdivision" passed by the planning board of our little Maine village. It was beginning to dawn on us that if it was that difficult in our own town, in our own country, where we understood the process and spoke the language, just *perhaps* we should reconsider undertaking a similar project in a new country, where we understood neither the language *nor* the laws and process.

So, the compromise idea that was beginning to shape up was to have enough land around us to not feel like we were in the middle of a "development" with neighbors visible all around us and that at least *might* offer the possibility of carving off a lot to sell in the future, but that wasn't so much land that it would *require* subdividing and re-selling portions just to be able to afford it.

Ben drove us around and showed us several pretty typical building lots of the type we'd already seen during the tour, and while we admired the view on several, none were even close to what we thought we wanted. We kept asking about "more acreage" while also recognizing that the $50,000 price that seemed typical for the 1-1/4 acre lots we were being shown was about the top of our theoretical budget (remember that "in theory" part about selling off our own lots back in Maine which was part of the foundation of whatever sense of "budget" we had) so we knew that we couldn't just pay the same "per acre" price for more acreage.

Ben did say he had some land that was still in its "pre-development" phase and that we could probably work out a deal for a larger parcel of that for a lower per acre price, but in the meantime we also stressed that it wasn't exactly that we were fixated on an actual specific *area* of land as much as we wanted the *feeling* that we got from having acreage. That is, we wanted the feeling that we weren't so close to our neighbors that we could see into their windows or smell what they were cooking for dinner. Possibly he had ideas, we speculated aloud, about land that would give us that feeling.

He began describing some land he had just outside San Ramon that was quite special, bordered by a river, with waterfalls and covered with jungle-y growth. (We'd tried to politely express our distaste for the barren hillsides we'd been looking at.) We asked if the land was *larger* than the other lots he'd shown us, and he said no, but it was somewhat more "private" feeling. It was near where we were at the moment, so we shrugged and said, "What the hell, let's just go look; it'll give us one more piece of "data" to put into our planning."

Famous last words.

Ben turned off the main highway and bounced mostly downhill for about five minutes, then turned onto a narrow minimal road that seemed to just disappear into the jungle. In only a moment we emerged into a clearing, a "plantel" that had been made to hold a future house. It was surrounded by trees and towering banana plants, but Ben waved off in a generally southwesterly direction and said that the Gulf of Nicoya was right through there. (We'd seen this same view from other lots, so we actually had a sense of what it looked like, even though at this point it was completely hidden behind the lush greenery.)

Notwithstanding David's aching swollen knee, we all set off to the river. It was a relatively easy walk down a more-or-less cleared path and after only a couple of minutes we found ourselves more deeply in the woods with a sense of dense shade and dampness as we approached the river.

We could clearly hear the roar of a waterfall and soon came to the end of the path right at the top of the falls. David and I both gave a collective gasp at the idea of actually living on this land, with this river, this waterfall, much less the two additional ones that Ben said made up the rest of the property border.

David looked at Ben and said, "No need to look any further. We'll take it!"

I looked at him long and hard. "It's only an acre and a quarter!" I pointed out. "*You're* the one who feels so strongly about not being on a little sub-division 'lot'—are you *sure* this is going to satisfy you?"

It wasn't that I didn't also love the land immediately. But I'd never had the same rigid idea that David had about not wanting to have near neighbors, or needing a large area of land around me, so I wanted to be sure that he wasn't just "falling in lust" as George often put it on the tour.

David said to Ben, "This is the land that George called your supercalifragilisticexpialidocious piece, isn't it?"

Ben looked blank for a moment, and then laughed. "I guess it could be, yes."

Now, David and I differ a bit on the exact details of this whole supercalifragilisticexpialidocious bit, but since it's *my* book, I get to tell it my way. I clearly remember George using this term to describe some of the available views available in Costa Rica, and in fact I know that he *still* uses it, so it's simply not possible that he meant it to apply to this one and only one piece of land.

David's version, however, has George applying the term singularly to this particular piece of land and although I do disagree with his assessment of *George's* use of the term, I really can't take any argument with his applying the term *to* this piece of land. If there were ever land that deserved Mary Poppin's magical description, this was it.

We agreed not to look any further for the day, figuring it would be hard after that to see anything else that we could even like, much less that we would feel so immediately and deeply connected to. Ben took us to lunch and then delivered us back to La Posada where we whiled away the rainy afternoon napping and reading and talking about the land.

We went back several times over the successive days to look at the land again, each time reaffirming how special it was. Even though we'd had **no** intentions of buying land on this trip—nor did we have any money with which to do so!—we signed an option with Ben that provided for us to pay $5,000 now and would give us until the end of the year to pay the balance. We felt sure we would have the house sale money by then and/or money from sale of one or more of our lots in Maine, so it seemed a pretty safe commitment on our part.

Now, I feel compelled to interrupt the story-telling a bit at this point and stress that I do NOT advise doing this. We did virtually EVERYTHING "wrong" according to all reasonable advice and the fact that it worked out well for us should not be taken as a recommendation to follow in our footsteps.

What, you say, did we do wrong? Let me count the ways:

- ❖ *Bought land on our first trip to Costa Rica*
- ❖ *Bought land without having rented here first to be sure the area was really where we wanted to be*
- ❖ *Bought land we didn't actually have the money in hand to buy*
- ❖ *Signed a contract written in Spanish prepared by the attorney of the seller, with no legal counsel of our own*
- ❖ *Did no research to confirm the seller's representation of the availability of water and electricity. (These should NEVER be assumed in Costa Rica.)*
- ❖ *Bought property bordered by a river with no clarification or verification of what the law would be regarding building near water*
- ❖ *Bought land two kilometers away from the paved road completely believing the seller's statement that the road was "going to be paved" soon*
- ❖ *Had no title search done or proof of actual "sub-dividing" of the "mother finca" (the original larger plot of land)*

Okay, now that I put it that way, we sound like complete idiots, and I suppose in many ways we were. I have to counter the confessions of all that stupidity, though, by ALSO saying we now own the land that we think is the most amazing we've ever seen in Costa Rica. We think it is vastly better than the "similar" lots we've seen around, and don't actually have a single moment of regret. So... what can I say? "Do as I say, not as I do" perhaps?

Had we done virtually any of the recommended items on the list above we might well not have bought this land. Not because of any intention to deceive on the part of Ben, as seller, but simply because it was early in the process of the sub-dividing of this particular piece of land and many of the reasonable "requirements" actually were not completed yet. Had we understood the issues of water and electricity we might have been scared off. A zealous attorney attempting to "protect" us could have easily made it seem that we were insane to go forward with this sale and talked us out of it.

So, in truth, I'm absolutely delighted that we did everything wrong. And maybe you'll find your perfect home, too, by doing things wrong. But I can't in good conscience advise it. So consider yourself properly forewarned.

Okay, back to our story.

Now we still had a number of days left in Costa Rica, but nothing left "to do" since we'd decided where to live, plus David's knee continued to cause him considerable pain. Our plan had been to rent a car for our treks back to Puriscal and over to Orosi, but those trips were now unnecessary.

As an alternative, we thought we might as well go ahead and squeeze in a bit of sightseeing, so we made plans to rent a car anyway, with me bravely saying no problem, I would drive. The rental car company brought the car to San Ramon and we met to go over the paperwork and make payment.

Uh oh. Turns out they didn't like that our "credit card" was, in fact, a debit card. We've rented cars readily over the years with our Visa debit card, so we were puzzled by the issue. We tried to explain that the company was actually *more* thoroughly protected since they could potentially access our entire bank account if there were a problem, whereas with a credit card they only had access to our credit limit, but rules were rules (odd in a country where rules often seem to be nothing more than *suggestions*) and we seemed to hit a brick wall.

As we sat there to ponder our options, which seemed to be pretty darn limited, it somehow came out that we could rent a *driver*—who in turn came with a car—by using our debit card. Do *not* ask me to explain why. I suppose in their view this had a more limited potential liability, but regardless of the logic (or lack thereof) behind it, the idea quickly grew on us.

In truth, my assertion that of course I could drive was more bravado than true bravery. I'd read so much about the terrible roads and drivers in Costa Rica that I wasn't honestly eager to be the one behind the wheel. So, plans were made and Nikolai, our English-speaking driver would pick us up first thing the following morning.

This turned out to be lucky for two reasons. One was simply that it really did turn out to be a much easier way to get around in a strange country where roads are primarily unmarked, maps of minimal use, and driving is challenging. The other is that by spending a couple of days with Nikolai, we discovered that we could also hire him to pick us up at the airport in a few months when we returned for good, so one more piece of the puzzle fell into place.

For a trip in which we hadn't planned to do any sightseeing at all, we managed over a couple of days to get a super clear view of Arenal Volcano, a quick jaunt to just *see* the Pacific Ocean which included the very cool opportunity to walk across the Tarcoles River Bridge with all the crocodiles below, and a bit of driving around just for generic sight-seeing.

We returned to Maine, David still limping, but with a huge sense of accomplishment and a solid enthusiasm for the upcoming move. We knew the next few months would be busy, but we were ready!

—Chapter 4

For us, our trip to Costa Rica confirmed that this was a good move for us. We had no second thoughts, no concerns that we might be making a terrible mistake, no fears other than just ironing out logistics. But it's not the same for everyone.

We were making this move simply because we *wanted* to. There was no particular *pressure* to move. Our becoming ex-patriots had been precipitated by a general conspiring of life events to make us open to the idea, but had not been prompted by any particular life crisis such as losing our jobs (as some friends had faced) or an acute financial crisis *forcing* us to seek a cheaper cost of living.

(We were attracted to the lower cost of living, since that meant I could afford to stop working at a regular full-time job, but we didn't feel like we *had to* move. Big difference!)

Something we didn't fully *think* about at the time, but we've since come to realize was a big *plus* for our easy adjustment here, is our experience over the years sailing in square-rigged ships. On the surface, there's not an obvious similarity. But moving to a foreign country and our sailing experiences shared more than would initially meet the eye.

Most importantly, living aboard a traditional ship you get used to a world that's completely different than the one you've always lived in up 'til then. A world where you're likely not to have most of the "normal" comforts of home, where you use a "foreign language" (sailing, especially in traditional ships, uses an extensive arcane vocabulary), and where most of your daily activities from using the toilet or showering to preparing and eating your meals will be done in a way that's simply *different* than you were used to on land. We'd lived in that weird world for weeks and months on end...and *liked* it.

This experience served us well. The adjustments that so many people speak of facing here in Costa Rica have simply not been a very big deal for us.

BUT—and it's a very big "but"—I daresay that most people who are thinking about moving to Costa Rica have *not* had the experience of living in their own strange floating world on board a sailing ship. Many, if not most, have *not* lived in *any* other "world" before, certainly not third world countries. Thus, for almost everyone, there will be some degree of culture shock and adjustment challenges.

If you've traveled to Costa Rica before as a tourist, you may feel like you *know* the country, but most folks find that the country they experienced as a tourist and the one they moved to might as well be on different planets, particularly if their past travels were on organized tours, or spending time primarily in resorts or vacation areas. So don't assume that because you've been to Costa Rica as a tourist that you'll automatically be exempt from the occasional hit of culture shock.

So, what are some of the possibly unexpected ways that life here is different?

One *should* be more obvious than it is: the language. Costa Rica is a Spanish speaking country. In almost all of the books you'll read about how many people speak English, many going so far as to suggest that you can get along just fine here if you don't speak Spanish. In my view, this is simply nuts. And wrong.

It *is* true that when you come here as a tourist you'll be able to *function* without speaking Spanish. Certainly the percentage of folks who speak *some* English is much higher in the tourist areas, although even then to expect that everyone is going to speak English is misguided. But you probably will get by.

I'd say it's equally true that you shouldn't *not move* to Costa Rica because you don't yet speak Spanish. But please, please, *please* make plans to learn at least some rudimentary Spanish. I'll tell you the truth—we *do* know people who have lived here for years who still speak almost no Spanish, but that simply boggles my mind. You guarantee that you are going to isolate yourself if you can't communicate, so why not learn? You may never become fluent, but that doesn't mean you shouldn't plan to learn what you can. Do you really want to be the embodiment of the "Ugly American" who expects everyone else to bend to *your* way of doing things?

We've found Ticos to be unfailingly kind in working with us to achieve *communication* even when we were clearly butchering their language. The overwhelming majority will listen intently, laboring mightily to imagine what you might be *trying* to say, prompt you with the word you're groping for, or go find someone—perhaps even in another store or house—who speaks some English. But without some degree of at least "survival" Spanish skills, everything you try to do will be much more difficult.

Even beyond the language, the simple fact that *doing* almost anything requires an entirely different level of effort and possibly headache than you're used to can be far more disorienting than you might expect. Despite some areas of surprisingly high sophistication— such as in the vast interlinked computer system for paying your bills almost anywhere!—the "systems" in

Costa Rica tend to be far more cumbersome than we're used to.

Buying something, for example, in almost any hardware store will require several steps of having one person assist you in identifying the item you want (which will often be hidden away securely behind a counter) and a second person to write up a sales slip which will either be manually or electronically transmitted to a "caja" or checkout where you will go pay for your purchase. The factura (receipt) will be printed and typically stamped and signed and all sorts of other fanfare before being given to you to present at yet another window or counter where you will finally be given your purchase.

There is a cultural expectation here that only a few employees can be trusted to handle money, that everyone is at least *possibly* attempting to steal something. Labor is inexpensive, and these multiple steps are seen as providing necessary checks and balances. While the arrival of Costa Rica's version of the "big box stores" (such as EPA, somewhat like a Home Depot, or Hipermas/Walmart) this multi-step process to purchase everything is slowly changing, but most small stores seem pretty determined to hang on to it, so be prepared! Making it easy for the customer is *not* a cultural expectation here.

In fact, the whole concept of "customer service" is not really built into the culture. Now, bear in mind, Costa Ricans are, generally speaking, a very polite and considerate people so it's not a matter of rudeness, but since almost *nothing* in their whole lives has happened quickly or efficiently, there's simply no orientation at all to that even being a goal.

As a result, *doing* things is a challenge. And you are likely to find yourself repeatedly puzzling over why things are done the way they are when it seems so *obvious*—to you!—that there is a much more efficient way. It's yet another unexpectedly disorienting characteristic to life here: efficiency simply isn't a prized quality, and we're not used to that. You might not think so, but this can feel downright weird.

So, is there anything you can do to prevent this culture shock? Or perhaps to make the decision that the differences would be too great for you and you're not a good candidate for this move?

From what I've seen in ourselves and others over the years, I think one big issue is to *know yourself!* Look at yourself (and your partner, if you have one) and pay attention to some key qualities:

❖ Have you experienced other situations in your life where the world as you knew it was turned upside down? If so, how did you react?

❖ How flexible are you? Do you tend to be amused and adaptable when things "go wrong" or are you tense and angry?

❖ How's your sense of time and space? Are you a so-called "Type A" personality? Does it make you feel a little crazy-annoyed when people are late or don't do what they promise?

❖ Do you meet new people easily?

❖ Are you flustered in unfamiliar situations? When facing something that feels completely "foreign" are you excited or fearful?

❖ Are you unhappy if you can't find your preferred brands, or do you just roll with the punches and pick out something different to try?

❖ How about food? Love to try new things or feel edgy and out of sorts if you can't have your favorites?

❖ Do you consider yourself patient? Do long lines make you tense?

❖ Do your children live across the street from you or across the country? Are you close? If you're used to spending lots of time with them now, how will you feel about only seeing them occasionally (and at some not-inconsiderable expense)?

I think you can probably pretty readily pick out the "better" answers in the questions above in terms of which qualities might help make the transition go *more* smoothly, but I think the point is not so much to say that one way is *good* and the other way is *bad*, but rather to *be aware* of areas where you might run into trouble.

Lots of "Type A" gringos have moved to Costa Rica and are very happy here—but they *knew* that about themselves and recognized that there would be challenges and they *wanted* to learn to be more relaxed in how they reacted to life.

And perhaps the most important aspect of culture shock is to simply recognize that even if you answer all the questions the "right" way, even if you think you're perfectly prepared for the move, you *might* still find some days when you want to hide in bed and pull the covers over your head. If you accept that as part of the process, you'll most likely be fine.

Notice that I'd mentioned earlier in this chapter about knowing yourself *and* your mate, if you're coming with one. I'm sure with many couples there might be one partner who is more "into" the idea than the other. Perhaps the more reluctant partner is concerned about moving so far away from friends and family, or is daunted more by the language barrier, or any number of other potential concerns. This is normal and in and of itself shouldn't be a reason not to make the move.

The key factor though, I believe, is the *degree* of difference in enthusiasm. When one partner is completely *driving* the decision and the other is significantly reluctant or, even worse, actively *against* the move, it is almost doomed to failure. This ranks right up there with "we'll have a baby to save our rotten marriage" as far as bad decisions go.

Despite how much we love Costa Rica, it would be unfair to imply that there aren't challenges and difficulties. For *us* those challenges are hardly blips on the radar; we're committed to this change in our lives and we believe that what we focus on increases, so we choose to focus not on the areas of difficulty but rather on the areas of delight, of which there are many!

However, and it's a big however, when one of you really doesn't want to be here, I can virtually guarantee that there will be countless opportunities to "reinforce" that feeling and every minor bump in the road will be felt like an earthquake.

We know of one couple where the wife really didn't want to come. She was afraid of the creepy-crawlies, so of course she opened her front door one day to find a snake coming to call on her.

She was terrified of the admittedly bad Costa Rican drivers and, sure enough, they narrowly missed being in a deadly accident. While stuck for hours in the resulting traffic, instead of focusing on appreciation for the fact that they *had* avoided any injury or damage themselves, she worked herself into a frenzy about how they were taking their lives into their hands every time they set foot out the door.

Construction on their new home wasn't even completed before they were already making plans to return to the U.S. It took them over a year to sell the new house, at a loss, and they wasted about $20,000 shipping all their worldly goods down and back again. And I shudder to even think about the ugly arguments that went on during their time here before agreeing to move back.

Other friends moved here despite the fact that he was a Viet Nam veteran actively struggling with Post Traumatic Stress Disorder (PTSD) and there were worries about continuing his treatment here. She was simply determined to make the move and pushed it through despite his concerns and objections, blindly hoping that once they were here it would be okay. He *wanted* to have it "be okay," but it really simply wasn't.

They moved back within two months, again having wasted more than $20,000 in shipping plus losing nearly another $4000 in pre-paid rent. (Dare we suggest that *pre-paying* rent under these circumstances might not have been the wisest choice? The 10% discount the landlord offered was nothing compared to the amount lost when they had to bail out on their lease.)

Does that mean you shouldn't make the move unless both of you are equally enthusiastic? Of course not. But be smart about it. Be one of the ones who actually *takes* the advice commonly given to *rent* before you *buy*. Although I think that normally shipping your household goods makes good sense, if you're one of the "divided" couples, leave it behind—in a storage unit if you have to—and rent a furnished house. The "extra" money you spend on rent and storage will be a drop in the bucket compared to the costs of shipping both ways.

Although it will often seem like the gringo world is made up of married couples, certainly many singles—both men and women—move to Costa Rica from the States. And many enjoy it thoroughly for all the reasons I've already given. But it's also true that some find that it's much harder being single in a foreign country far away from their traditional support structure of work and friends and family and often not even speaking the same language (at least not fluently) as the locals.

In some cases, singles of both genders come looking for love. Unfortunately—at least for single gringo women—many of the men come looking for a young Tica to share their lives. Whereas I don't think we knew anyone in the States, certainly no one within our immediate circle, who was married to a woman less than half his age, we know a number of them here.

I don't mean to make it sound like they're some kind of lecherous old men—they're friends, they're nice guys. There's just a different social structure here and this is a more typical situation which can be pretty frustrating to the over-50 single woman who sees all the "eligible men" around her hooking up with Ticas younger than their daughters. So, no judgment here, just something to consider if you're a single woman who's coming to Costa Rica hoping to find a man.

Now, for singles of either gender, you're not alone (so to speak) and I sure wouldn't let "single-hood" keep me from moving here if I were so inclined. We have single men and women friends who are delighted to be here, so "come on down"—just be aware that there is the *chance* that being single in a foreign country *might* make you feel more isolated than you would at home in your own familiar environment.

And speaking of isolation, after being here several years now and seeing who does and doesn't adjust easily and happily, I'd have to say that isolation can be a major factor. And although it seems obvious looking at it from the outside, and with the wisdom of hindsight, it certainly wasn't obvious to the folks in question or you can be sure they would have made other choices.

That land with the beautiful view might not be such a great deal if it means that you'll be stuck with no internet or phone service, down a treacherous road that you're scared to drive on.

The house that was a great price out in the country in a Tico neighborhood may feel much less like a bargain when you find that you sit alone in your house, isolated from any neighbors who speak the same language, without even having television available other than through a very pricey satellite service.

Is all land with a beautiful view going to result in that kind of isolation? Are all bargain Tico houses a bad idea? Absolutely not!

And for some folks, those very characteristics just might describe their ideal life. But for others, they can result in an increased feeling of "culture shock" and unhappiness, even depression. Isolation is a powerful thing and its impact shouldn't be underestimated.

So one thing to think about as you plan your move is how will you meet other people? Do you have enough Spanish to jump right into developing a strong Tico social circle or will you want some other gringos around? For ourselves, we knew that we did *not* want to live in a gated community surrounded only by other gringos. But at the same time, we also knew we wanted to have *some* other folks who spoke English and who shared some of our experience of leaving our homes and moving to a foreign country as well as simply a more common background.

We've found that we have more friends here in Costa Rica than we had after twenty years of living in Maine. But we have had essentially a built-in system for meeting new people by the common denominator of those who had taken "the George tour" as we all call it. If you *don't* have any identified way to meet new people, you *might* find that the resulting isolation isn't peaceful and relaxing, but just plain lonely. Just something to think about.

Is there any magical set of factors that will guarantee that you'll be happy if you move to Costa Rica? Unfortunately not. I can actually offer that, somewhat "counter-intuitively," there is a factor that will work *against* your being happy here, and that is if you're unhappy where you currently are.

Sure, I think that many people looking to make this move might experience *some* type of unhappiness in their current life—I mean, if your life is perfect where it is, why are you considering moving? But if you are experiencing a more deeply rooted sense of unhappiness, it can be a mistake—a tragic mistake even—to think that a simple change of scenery will solve your problems. As the old saying goes, wherever you go there you are.

So, turning that to the positive, I can offer that your likelihood of "successfully" moving to Costa Rica is much greater if you are fundamentally content with your life, but there are some aspects that would be improved by such a move. Perhaps, as we experienced, you're tiring of cold winters (or blisteringly hot summers) and the weather is a big attraction. Perhaps you're seeking a lower cost of living so that you can relieve some financial stress.

While in most places Costa Rica is no longer "cheap" the way it might have been twenty years ago, it is also true that *most* folks moving to Costa Rica from the U.S. or Canada will find that they can live a far more comfortable lifestyle on less money than they can "up north." For many, the simple savings in utility costs— not having to either heat or cool their homes—can be enough to make the difference between their income providing a comfortable lifestyle or one filled with scrimping and financial anxiety.

For others, the idea of a new life adventure can be a compelling reason to consider moving to Costa Rica—for them there's nothing *wrong* with their existing life, they just see that there could be something even *better* by trying out a new one.

So, like most of life, there's no single answer as to whether Costa Rica will be right for you. And even if it's *right* for you for a time, doesn't mean it will always be. Yes, there are some people who move down and move back quite immediately. I've mentioned a couple of examples of that.

But others come down and live quite happily for some years, and still find that the time comes when they prefer to be "back home." It's not an endurance contest. There's nothing at all that says you can't simply move back at some point if you want. (Or, for that matter, move somewhere else entirely.)

It's interesting, in fact, that the words "succeed" or "successful" are often used when talking about moving to Costa Rica. (And, yes, I realize that even *I* said "successfully" a page or so ago.) These words automatically put the whole idea of moving here into a kind of competition—can you "make it" here, will you "succeed" in your efforts to adjust, or will you "fail" and go home again?

The odd part is that we—as a "people" in North America—tend to move around a lot. It's not the slightest bit uncommon to move across the country for a job promotion or a career change. People get divorced, they get married, they have babies, their children grow up and move away—all situations where moving from one place to another is taken for granted as part of the natural evolution of life. Almost no one says things like, "Sheesh, they couldn't cut it living in Ohio and went running back to Virginia!"

So why do we do that when it comes to living in Costa Rica? You may remember that I told earlier how, when I was doing my own research, I was just horrified whenever I found out that someone who moved to Costa Rica had moved "back" again. I think I simply didn't want to even *consider* the possibility that this move would not be everything we were hoping. Now that I've been here for a while, I can better relax and acknowledge that some people move here very happily, and *still* they move again at some point in the future. (See the "More Useful Stuff" section at the back of this book for a few firsthand stories written by folks who moved here, then moved back again.)

But, the first thing you need to know is whether you even want to move here in the first place, and then how to go about it. Hopefully one thing you *will* get out of this book and from reading about our experiences is enough information to help you know—as well as anyone *can* prior to actually *doing* it—whether this is a move you want to make.

For us, our ten days in Costa Rica confirmed our belief that it was a move *we* wanted, so the next three months flew by as we turned our somewhat crazy idea into a true plan.

—Chapter 5

Okay, primed for success, ready to go! What do we do next?

This is where we found ourselves after our return to Maine. Now that we'd confirmed our intention to move to Costa Rica, the *real* process of making plans began. All the research until this point was focused, in some ways, on *whether* it made sense for us to move to Costa Rica. Now we needed to move beyond the *ifs* and the *whys* and into the *hows.*

Finances were a major issue in our planning, as I'm sure they must be for many. A couple of years earlier, after much analysis of pros and cons, David had begun drawing his social security at age 62. (It was that very fact of his being retired that had made it possible for us to have my parents move up to Maine from Louisiana when it became clear that they needed daily assistance.)

As long as we lived in Maine, though—or probably anywhere in the U.S.—his social security was barely a drop in the bucket toward covering our expenses and my working full time, earning a minimum of $50,000 and ideally more, was an absolute necessity. Part of the goal in moving to Costa Rica would be for me to *not* have to work so that I could spend more time taking care of my folks in their final years.

My parents had been in academia their whole lives. My dad was a professor and department chair in the small private liberal arts school, Centenary College, in Louisiana and my mom was a private piano teacher. Later, after we kids were older, she, too, taught at Centenary. Earnings were modest but they'd raised a family of three kids, paid off a home, traveled extensively, and managed a frugal but comfortable lifestyle.

More impressive, though, was that they'd managed to save money during their working years and now had a couple of annuities to supplement their social security, plus a bit of money invested in mutual funds.

This was in somewhat of a direct contrast to David and me, who had salaries at various points in our careers that probably surpassed anything my parents had earned, but had no savings, no investments, and no retirement funds other than David's social security of a little over $1,000 a month.

(Lordy, it sounds pretty pitiful when you actually put it down in black and white like that, doesn't it? On the other hand, I think we're not entirely alone in our generation in being in this unfortunate condition. We had actually once inherited a fairly large sum of money from David's father, but had "invested" it all in an ambitious non-profit project that had ended up going belly-up after almost a decade of effort. So in our meager defense it wasn't entirely "our fault" that we were now penniless. But that's another story entirely.)

Through combining his social security with what my parents had, we would be looking at a monthly income of a bit over $5,000 for the 4 of us. While the majority of that would "belong" to my parents, their capacity to cover many of our major living expenses would be offset by our being their caregivers as the years went by, a role that was already taking on more importance and effort just in the past year and a half that we'd been doing it.

It's easy to hear that Ticos often live on $500 or less a month and think, *how could you not live like royalty on 10-times that?!?,* but we were also realistic enough to know instinctively that a lifestyle afforded by $500 a month, or even many times that, was not one that was likely to satisfy us—or, frankly, *many* gringos!

We didn't live luxuriously in Maine, by any means, but we *did* enjoy eating good food and entertaining fairly often. We had wine regularly in the evenings, like to buy books, and we consider high speed internet to be a necessity along with (I'm a little embarrassed to report) decent TV service. Our abundance of pets assured regular veterinarian bills, not to mention medical expenses for the "senior" portion of our family (which was, after all, three-quarters of us!).

We also were a family of *four* (plus the four animals), not the more typical couple or single person. So while there would be some "economies of scale" since we only needed one house, on the other hand it had to be a bigger than average house to hold all of us comfortably. Many significant expenses—food and medical, most notably—were truly "times four" in our case.

I spent countless hours researcing costs of living in Costa Rica, at least as best as I could. This wasn't as easy as I wished.

Unfortunately, most of us were raised with some variation on the rule of etiquette that says you don't talk about money. You don't talk about how much you make or ask others about their income. You don't ask someone how much something costs, what they paid to build their home, or what they spend on their electric bill every month. Generally speaking, you just *don't do it.*

But, when you're trying to ascertain whether such a radical change in lifestyle is possible, how can you do it unless people *talk* about the very things they were told their entire lives it was impolite to discuss?!?

Luckily, this dichotomy seemed to be recognized by at least *some* folks who had already moved to Costa Rica and we found that with diligence and continued research we were able to find enough references to the various expenses we were likely to encounter to draw up proposed budgets.

(See the "More Useful Stuff" section at the back of this book for our budgets that we'd developed at the time, as well as a current listing of our monthly expenses.)

But, first, we had some fundamental decisions to make: Should we take the frequently offered advice to rent for a while before moving lock, stock, and barrel? Should we rent our house out in Maine before selling it in case we found that it didn't work out and we wanted to return? Should we go down to Costa Rica for a few months and plan to come back to Maine for the final moving process?

Each of these options affected many things, of course, certainly not least of which was finances. In the early months of planning, we thought it would make the most sense to take a conservative approach—go for a few months and rent, make sure it was all we were hoping, then come back to Maine and attend to the details of selling the house, shipping our household goods, and "wrapping up" our life in the states. I have to say that I still do think this is a reasonable approach.

In our case, though, the more we *planned* and the further we got *into* our plans, the more inclined we were to just jump in with both feet. This was partly emotional—we just wanted to *get there* and start this new life!— and part of it was practical and financial.

While we were still blissfully unaware of the impending real estate crash, we *were* aware that Brunswick Naval Air station—a significant contributor to the economy of our community—had just been put on the dreaded military base closure list and that would mean that a whole mess of houses would be dumped on the market over the next couple of years as they phased out the base.

We began to feel that, ironically, the more prudent option might actually be to sell our house now when we could hopefully still get a good price for it, as well as the house-lots in the small sub-division we'd made from our eighteen acres of property around the house. This would give the best chance of having a chunk of capital with which to build a new house in Costa Rica, free and clear of a mortgage payment, buy the things we felt like we needed like a 4-wheel drive car, and still keep a little cushion in the bank.

Surely that fits into the "best laid plans…" category. (I'll spare you the suspense and give you the punch line right away, which is that we **never** were able to sell the Maine property; the bank eventually foreclosed although it took them years to do so.) But even though things didn't work out like we planned, they still "worked out"—just in a different way since we're here in Costa Rica now and wouldn't have it any other way.

We did manage to capture some of the equity in our house, although I nearly screwed that up just through simple ignorance of how home financing works. We put our house on the market quickly, wanting to allow as much time as possible for it to sell before we left. *Then* we realized that maybe it would be better to go ahead and *refinance* so that we could have some cash in hand by the time we wanted to move even if the house hadn't closed yet.

(At that point we weren't even considering the possibility that the house wouldn't sell at all, but it did seem likely to think that even with a buyer in hand, we could be waiting another month, two, or even three for a closing.)

So we approached a big mortgage company about refinancing the house. At that time we had a mortgage of around $160,000 and the house had appraised the previous year at $330,000 so it seemed reasonable that there was some decent money to be had there.

The application was going along swimmingly until it was discovered that the property was listed on the MLS (Multiple Listing Service) listings for sale. Oops.

Turns out you can't finance a home that's for sale! Why not? Didn't make sense to me, but it was explained to me that the lenders don't *want* the loan paid off in just a few months. They don't make enough money that way. Who knew?

Okay. I tried explaining it away that we'd just put it on the market to "test the waters" and we pulled it right off again, but the damage was done. We tried one of those services that claims to find you a lender among many possibilities, but no dice. No refinancing. I was bummed.

We weren't about to give up, although I'll admit the answer didn't seem immediately apparent.

With the budgets that we'd worked up, we felt confident that we could afford our monthly living expenses in Costa Rica from the various pensions coming into the family, but the costs of actually *making* the move would need a chunk of capital that we didn't have.

Except sitting in our house.

(And, again, it might be important to remember that this was 2006, following years of outrageous real estate market growth just *before* the collapse, and it truly hadn't yet occurred to us that this chunk of capital

84

we envisioned might not actually *exist* except on paper and in our imaginations!)

It's also important to note that what has taken me less than two *pages* to describe here, actually took place over two *months*, which meant we were marching closer and closer to our desired moving date without yet having solved this key financial issue.

Serendipitously we got a promotional insert in our bank statement about their home equity line of credit (LOC) loans. Hmmm.... maybe this was a route to go. Didn't seem likely that we could get quite *as much* of the equity since there were different rules and all that, but if we weren't greedy then maybe we could get enough to ensure that we could actually make the move as planned.

Luckily, the home equity LOC idea worked, and we had access to up to $50,000 in time to buy the plane tickets (a not-inconsequential $5,000 expense for the four of us), pay for the shipping, purchase all our packing materials, and feel like we had a little money "in the bank" so to speak. Whew!

While we worked at sorting out the "lump sum" money issue, we also continued our overall, general planning. Timing was a big issue. Now that we'd decided to move for sure, we were eager to get going. But we knew from our investigations that we wouldn't be able to fly with our dogs and cats until after the end of the summer moratorium at the airlines. So that essentially dictated a post-September 15 move. From there, we fantasized about end of September or early October, but practical realities began to suggest mid-to-late October as the magic window of opportunity.

At least I could relax that our shipping uncertainties seemed to be over. We were very pleased with George's recommendation for Ship Costa Rica, and in mid-August I emailed Barry to officially begin the process, inquire about a specific quote, and get the details about how to pack, make our inventory, etc. Although it took him several days (and a second inquiry) to answer my initial email, we continued to have a good feeling about both his prices and just his general competence. We felt confident that we were in good hands.

We resigned ourselves to sending two 40' containers, but contrary to our initial thinking we decided to include my parents' car in one of them. Ironically, I didn't begin to know then what I know now about the difficulties of buying a good quality car in Costa Rica, but what I *did* begin to more fully realize was how well my parents' Ford minivan suited them.

With my dad's Parkinson's Disease, he was still mobile but didn't get around *easily*. The front seat of the minivan was just the right height to minimize his discomfort and effort getting in and out of the car. The

Windstar was large enough to carry all four of us and still have room for purchases or luggage or the dogs. It was more than ten years old, so although we didn't fully understand the process or costs of importing a car, we did grasp that its value would be pretty low, so the cost to import it would accordingly be pretty low as well.

So, now we had a plan of sorts—load two containers in early October so that they could begin their several-week-long trek to Costa Rica. We felt like we could manage to "camp out" at home with the "leftovers"—the things we weren't planning on taking with us—for a couple of weeks. That would let the containers with all the rest of our stuff be halfway through their journey by the time we actually flew down to Costa Rica, thus giving us only another couple of weeks before things would be there and ready for us.

By early September, though, we were seeing time slipping away (remember that all this time we were dealing with the efforts to acquire the necessary hunk of capital to even *pay* for shipping these two containers) and let Barry know that we were thinking of postponing our move until late October or even sometime in November. He encouraged us to load the containers by the end of October in order to be assured of having our stuff cleared through customs and ready for us before things all shut down for the Christmas holidays.

That was just enough of a kick in the butt to get us back on track for a late October move. As the money got sorted out right about then as well, things seemed to be falling into place.

One of the last issues, at least for *this* particular phase of the move, was breaking the news at work and making a plan for an organized exit. As I mentioned earlier, during the many months of our investigations and research I hadn't said anything at work about our plans. I had struggled to find the right balance between being fair to my employer while also ensuring my own financial survival by not being forced out of my job too far ahead of our move which is what I feared would happen once they knew.

I had to make *some* explanations when I went on my exploratory trip to Costa Rica, especially since it meant taking more time off than the minimal one week of vacation to which I was entitled and that was unusual enough in our company to require a good reason.

At the time I settled on as close a version of the truth as seemed possible: that we were considering retiring to Costa Rica and wanted to go check it out. I explained that the pressing need to do this *now* was because we needed to begin planning for this future event, that it would affect certain decisions we needed to make now, and we couldn't know whether it was a viable idea or not until we went there.

I'm a fundamentally honest person and, frankly, I didn't like lying to my colleagues and boss. I worked for a small, family-owned company, so it wasn't like dealing with some vast anonymous corporation, but rather real people I knew and liked and had spent a majority of my waking hours with over the past several years.

But, at the same time, I couldn't risk revealing my plans and having them tell me to go ahead and leave (before I was ready), so that was the best I could come up with. It was, in fact, essentially true. It was only the *timetable* that I wasn't being quite honest about. (Okay, it was the timetable that I wasn't being *at all* honest about, if you want to be picky about it!)

Once I'd returned from our trip, I enthusiastically told people at work that we loved Costa Rica, that we'd bought land and were, indeed, making plans to retire there. I just didn't clarify that we were moving in three months, not three years.

As the time grew closer to our actual planned departure, it got to the point where I absolutely had to give notice. I worked it out to tell them about six weeks ahead of our anticipated travel date, and tried to explain that the more we'd worked the numbers and talked about the idea of "retiring" to Costa Rica, the more it became clear to us that we should not hold off for years but, rather, *do it now.*

I used our belief that this move would be good for my parents to help bolster support for this rather radical-seeming timing change and again, that was essentially true. Certainly moving to a climate that would be good for my folks year 'round, where we could afford to hire people to help us with them, had been a big motivator from the beginning!

I emphasized my desire to tell them right away, as soon as we'd decided (okay, God's gonna get me for *that* little lie) so that I could work for the next six weeks to "tidy things up" as much as possible. That way, their handling my clients after I left would be as easy as possible for them. Other than taking a bit of time off in the middle to pack up and actually load the shipping containers, I committed to work up until then and also come back after that right up until we left to give as much time as I could to this tidying process.

Thankfully, they were comparatively good-natured about it. Right away they wanted me to stop seeing new clients, which was understandable but put an odd crimp in my day since much of what I ordinarily did was meet with walk-ins and talk with people on the phone, both activities which were now off-limits to me. Everyone in the office was pleasant but there was this odd quality of suddenly being shunted off to the side of the business.

One thing was clear. Had I given six months notice instead of six weeks, I had no doubt that once I had transferred my paperwork on existing accounts to my colleagues, there would have been no further reason to keep me on. So while I still felt guilty about basically lying to them for months—by *omission* if nothing else—I could also tell that I'd done the right thing.

At least now the deed was done and we could stop being so secretive about our plans. That was a relief.

Unfortunately, another important "telling people" situation had *not* gone so well and relief would be slow in coming. Perhaps my sad tale about "breaking the news" to my family—most specifically my brother—will give you some food for thought about how you can best approach the subject with *your* family.

When we first had this idea and began researching, I knew it sounded pretty "out there." Despite having a relatively sophisticated, educated, and well-traveled set of friends, we knew no one who had retired to a foreign country. So I wanted to do a good bit of research first to assure myself that it really was a sane idea before we told others.

As time went on and we began to make plans, the few folks that we did tell all greeted the news enthusiastically. We discovered that many people we knew absolutely loved Costa Rica—it had just never come up in previous conversations. For those who didn't really know much about Costa Rica, as we hadn't, we were able to offer the insights we'd gained in our research—great weather, excellent medical care, high literacy rate, peaceful democracy without an army.... "What's not to like?" it seemed to us.

It never occurred to me to *hide* our plans from my brother, because it never occurred to me that he would object.

But, likewise, it somehow just never came up in the first months of our investigations and eventual planning. We talked on the phone pretty regularly, but usually really focused around his chatting with Mom and Dad as he'd always done over the years. It perhaps sounds implausible, but I truly just never thought to mention it.

(Can you feel the "uh oh" that's coming?!?)

So, after we'd been researching for several months and had really gotten enthusiastic about the idea, we talked with Hans about his coming to Maine to stay with Mom and Dad so that we could make our exploratory trip to Costa Rica. Without "pre-planning" any kind of strategy we just blurted out the plans, focused on the logistics of his needing to come to Maine, *not* on the issues of *whether* we should even be considering such a move.

To say he was stunned would be an understatement. It had been David who'd actually talked with him that first time and he called me immediately afterwards at work to report that he thought I would *really* need to follow up with Hans since he seemed rather upset. I don't think David specifically had realized that I'd never mentioned it to Hans until he ran smack dab into Hans' sputtering response.

The worst of it was simply that Hans and I had *never* in all our lives actually fought about anything, certainly nothing beyond childhood squabbling. He was deeply hurt that I seemingly hadn't considered his feelings about taking my parents so far away and despite long and heartfelt emails from me trying to explain my thinking and apologize for the apparent oversight, his anger and hurt were slow to dissipate.

He didn't actively stand in our way, but I'm not entirely sure that we'll ever completely get past it, which saddens me greatly. Until recently, I've often said that that was one of my only "mistakes" in planning our move—not telling Hans about the idea right from the start and getting his input—but I actually have come to see that as painful as it was (and is), perhaps it worked out for the best after all.

He was so adamantly against it, I'm afraid that had I come up face-to-face with his objections earlier in the process, he might have actually persuaded me not to do it. And *that* would have been a real sadness since we love it here so much and it's been such a great place to care for my parents. So, who's to say which would have been better? Since I can't change the past anyway, I'll never know.

I share this story with you mostly to encourage *you* to think: who in your life is going to be affected by this move? Just as with me, your employer (if you have one) is obvious. Friends and family will be affected, too, possibly more than you originally thought.

For many, leaving their children or their parents behind is a difficulty. If you're of retirement age (using the term very loosely) then almost by definition your children, if you have them, will be young adults and your parents, if you have them, will be old. Your children, in most cases, will manage fine on their own, but depending on how *close* you currently are—physically—you may find moving away to be challenging.

In our case, our son Collin and our daughter Jen had already moved cross-country and were living at opposite ends of California, so our move to Costa Rica put them physically closer, if anything. And they were more than happy with the idea of coming to visit us in Costa Rica as opposed to simply flying "home" to Maine, which—by their standards—was pretty boring.

And our parents were a non-issue as far as moving *away* from them, since we were taking them with us. (David's parents had passed some years before, so it was only my parents to be concerned with.) But for many, elderly parents, perhaps with failing health, are a *big* issue, and actually one that frequently takes people *back* to the U.S after they've moved here.

While our more casual friends were cheerful about our plans—perhaps, like our kids, looking forward to having someone now to go visit in Costa Rica!—some of our closer friends were more taken aback and not quite so cheerful.

My closest girlfriend for many years lived in Nova Scotia, and her family had driven down to spend vacations with us annually, sometimes even more frequently, for more than the past decade, actually nearly two. Our moving so far away from them was a sadness.

Our dear friends, Jon and Bethany, too, found the planned move to be disconcerting to them. Although we'd been friends for many years while they'd lived in Rhode Island, they'd only moved to Maine comparatively recently and we'd enjoyed spending time together. They lived an hour or so away from us, further down the coast, and it wasn't uncommon for us to go to one another's houses for the weekend just to hang out, enjoy good meals, and relax.

They never directly said anything (what was there to say, after all?) but there was a chill to the relationship after we told them of our plans. Simply sorry to see us leave, I think, and "missing us" even before we'd left. They absolutely stepped up to the plate, though, with a final act of friendship by coming to our house essentially in the middle of the night with Jon's huge F-350 truck and Bethany's station wagon to schlep us, our nineteen suitcases, four humans, and four pet crates to the airport for a 4 am arrival! Now *that's* friendship, especially since at some level I'm sure they felt they were *facilitating* the very thing they were unhappy to see happen.

So, any final advice? Perhaps not really, other than to just help you be aware that none of us live in a vacuum, and your planned move to Costa Rica is likely to affect more people than you might realize. You might take a little time to think about who you need to talk with directly (as opposed to having them hear it second-hand), how to best approach them, and be respectful that they might not be nearly as enthusiastic about your move as *you* are!

And WHY, you might ask, was my brother so opposed to our move? Part of it was emotional—the very fact that I hadn't considered his opinion when he, too, had always been close to our parents was simply hurtful. Not logical, since I explained in great depth how unintended that was and that I actually had simply never thought he'd object, but emotions are not always logical, are they?

Another major factor was financial. We had spent quite a bit of money moving my parents up to Maine the previous year, had invested a substantial sum (of their money) in renovating the garage into an art and music studio for them, and now were going to leave all that behind. It seemed financially reckless to Hans. I think he feared that if our decision to move them to Maine had not proven to be wise—as we now seemed to be saying, otherwise why were we planning to move!—why should he expect our decision to move them to Costa Rica to be any wiser.

Lastly, actually unknown to me until that time, his wife had done her college work in Latin American studies. She was strongly convinced that NO Latin American country is truly stable or could possess the characteristics that we cited in support of our move over the long haul. While we didn't—and don't—share her opinion, I have to admit it was sincerely held on her part, and she had convinced my brother as well, so that his objections came from genuine concern.

—Chapter 6

Right on schedule we approached the San Jose airport. Costa Rica lay lush and green beneath us, just as promised in all the tourist literature. David nudged me. "What's that water?" he asked with a puzzled look.

I aimed my exhausted, bleary eyes out the window to see a long chunk of blue water. I pondered.

"It's gotta be Lake Arenal, don't you think? I'm pretty sure that's the only water that big in this general area. Do you see a volcano nearby?" I wouldn't have thought we passed over Arenal coming from Atlanta but, frankly, my sense of Costa Rican geography was still pretty fuzzy.

More craning to see out the window and David exclaimed, "Yes, there it is! Don't you see it? It's steaming!"

It was gone from view before I got a look, but it still made me smile to know it was out there. We don't have many volcanoes in Maine.

It was a little past 12:30 in the afternoon, Tico-time, otherwise known as Central Standard Time. We had flown out of Portland, Maine at 6:30 that morning,

Eastern Daylight Time, or almost exactly 8 hours before. Despite the botched-up transfer in Atlanta where they hadn't arranged for the wheelchair for Daddy, the flights themselves had gone smoothly, including the bonus of having cushy "Business Class" service on the long leg from Atlanta to San Jose. But the day had sure begun anything but smoothly. In fact, very little of the past week had gone smoothly.

Two weeks earlier, only a few days before we were scheduled to load our first container, we had asked to postpone when the weather forecast predicted hard rain on both our Thursday and Friday loading days.

This was a hard decision to make since we'd wanted to get our stuff *on its way* to Costa Rica in order to minimize our waiting time for it once *we* arrived. We'd also really looked forward to having the 10 days between loading and departure for a little "breathing room" to attend to odds and ends of final business.

But once we postponed the loading we'd also breathed a big sigh of relief since deep down I think we both felt like we couldn't possibly have been ready to load in two days. The extra week now felt like a real gift.

I'd been coolly confident that the packing would come together in the two weeks we'd allowed, but I'd grossly misjudged. I hadn't adequately taken into account how much longer it takes to pack things for international shipping versus a short drive across town, or even across the country.

The little bit of extra time per item doesn't seem like much, until you multiply it times the hundreds (thousands?) of items we were packing. An international move will definitely cause you to re-think your habits of collecting crystal, dishware, and other assorted breakables—as I am wont to do.

We had also acquired so much extra stuff over the past few years when David's mother had lived with us, before her passing, and now with my parents living with us. Somehow all those extra things had managed to blend into our house, so it was easy to pretend they weren't there, but packing time proved they really *were* there. Lots of them.

With the container loading postponed we eased up a bit on the packing frenzy, but still continued to plod along every day, getting more and more boxes packed up and moved down to the studio. We were lucky to have this converted garage down closer to the road, which would be the "loading zone" for the container. With two tight 90-degree turns on the approach to the house, the container would only be able to pull in the very first leg of the driveway. Having the studio let us move things out of the house and have them ready and close-by for the eventual loading.

Each day the detailed inventory grew and the house looked ever-so-slightly less full. It was the *ever-so-slightly* part that worried me a little, since it seemed by now that the house should be looking *really empty* and I can't say that was the case. Sure, if you looked closely you could see that bookcases were devoid of books and walls were now bare since our artist friend, Billy McNamara, had generously flown in from Arkansas and spent an entire week packaging the artwork for shipping. And a few spare pieces of furniture had even been moved down to the studio which would serve as a staging area for loading.

The vast amount of stuff *remaining* in the house a few days before the loading *should* have given me a clue that we were going to be in trouble. But I clung optimistically to the view that it would be all right, that we'd be ready in time, especially now that we had an entire extra week.

One additional wrinkle in the plan was that since we'd thought the containers would be loaded and on their way by now, I'd made the promise to return to my job for a final week. This would give me a chance to tie up some loose ends, most notably wrapping up some of the detailed prep work for my most complex client.

Now, of course, since we were still packing, my heading off to the office every day was inconvenient, to say the least. But I'd made the commitment and while I already knew I probably wouldn't get those ends tied up as tightly as I'd hoped, I wasn't prepared to just bail on the company, or my word.

So I went in to the office early each morning, then came home around 5 or 6 and packed for a while, then fixed dinner, then packed some more, and finally tumbled exhausted into bed, to repeat it all the next day.

We'd planned that I would be finished with my work on Thursday the 19th of October since we were now loading up container #1 on Friday the 20th, but on Thursday evening I realized I still had another hour or two of work. So I headed home, promising to come back one last time before we flew the following Wednesday.

I'd even (oh so naively) reported that I thought the first container would fill up pretty easily with the couple hundred boxes we already had packed, plus my parents' minivan which would take up nearly half the length, so I might even be back in the office on Friday afternoon.

Can we say, "Not!"

After postponing the previous week due to impending rain, it—of course—also rained on Friday, when there was no further time for postponement.

Thankfully, the rain was mostly just the spitting and drizzling variety, with the true *downpour* holding off until we were nearly finished.

Like many moves, the initial phase seemed to go so smoothly that we were lulled into thinking this wouldn't be too bad. Nine hours later we knew we'd been bamboozled.

We headed out at 7:30 in the morning to get the rental pick-up truck in Brunswick, planning on using it to shuttle things from the house to the container. (The container could only barely pull into the first leg of the driveway, not maneuver around the two 90 degree turns necessary to get to the front door.) No problems there; we were soon on our way with a shiny new pick-up truck.

While David drove the truck home, I went to Dunkin' Donuts for a Box o' Joe, some hot chocolate, and donuts for our work crew. (The temperature was still in the 40s and we were pretty sure some hot coffee and chocolate would be welcomed back at the house.)

David also suggested I get breakfast sandwiches for us there as well. But our local Dunkin' Donuts was noted for its staff moving at the speed of cold molasses, and by the time I'd rounded up the coffee and donuts I was about to lose it completely and possibly murder the girl behind the counter (which at the very least would almost certainly interfere with our plans to move to

Costa Rica). So I headed just a bit down the road to McDonalds—where "fast food" was actually fast—for a bunch of breakfast-to-go, some of which David and I would eat right away and some of which could be reheated a little later for Mom and Dad.

When I got home the first of our moving helpers, Dave and Raylene's son, Chris, was at the house. (Although Dave and Raylene lived only a few miles away from us in Maine, we'd only recently met when Barry had called to ask if we would be willing to put a couple of recliners for them in one of our containers. They, too, were moving to Costa Rica but weren't planning on sending a container.) Our friend Steve was also there, dismantling the sliding "barn door" on the studio which we wanted to open to facilitate the move. (It had been closed in behind a "removable" wall during the studio renovation.)

Soon the piano movers arrived, thankfully with three hefty men since much of the "muscle" we'd promised to have on hand had, so far, failed to materialize. They went right to work and by 9:30 had the grand piano ready to load onto the container.

Just about then the truck driver showed up to pull the container out of the middle of the yard where he'd stowed it overnight and the loading was officially underway, although we were still missing the majority of our work crew. We'd had problems these past two days with them failing to show up as expected, so we were a bit nervous although David had talked with them this morning and they had sworn they were "on the way."

In response to the drizzle, I was sent the few miles into Richmond to the hardware store to acquire a large tarp, where I bought two just for good measure. The larger one we rigged up from the top of the container over to the front edge of the studio (where it was just screwed right into the outer wall). We then stretched it out and attached it to the dumpster and the tall post of our lawn umbrella to create an awning which proved to be very successful, if a bit ragtag looking.

Without giving a blow-by-blow description of the rest of the day, I think the best I can say is that we survived it. Patrick and his friends (our "worker fellows") showed up eventually and boxes began to move quickly into the container. After the first hour, though, we hit a wall where we fully understood the difference between setting the boxes into the container vs. actually *loading* everything in a solid mass that wouldn't move as the container ship slogged its way through a few thousand miles of ocean. That slowed things down considerably.

Meanwhile the clock was ticking so David called his pal at the local high school and arranged for four more athletic young fellows to appear after their half day at school. (Who knows *why* it was a half day, but our good fortune it was.) It turned out to be slight overkill, but not by much. And they were all going to be available for the 2nd container loading in another couple of days when many bodies would be very helpful, since that load would be mostly furniture.

Although I'd optimistically figured that the packed boxes would just about fill up the container space to the point where we would load the van, it became clear that there would be a good bit of empty space. So the move was on to start loading the "big stuff"—the real furniture—to pack us up solid.

Thank goodness I'd bought some of that magic "sticks only to itself" plastic stuff that they wrap furniture and boxes in. Whew, it's cool stuff and before long we had the sofa and love seat wrapped up and they joined the carefully padded and wrapped china cupboard and stereo speakers that our helpers had prepared the day before. Although a frantic call had gone out for "more stuff" at one point, it turned out that those things plus the new (used) hot tub actually did fill the space.

Bear in mind that as we loaded, each and every item put in the container had to have a number, which had to match the detailed inventory sheet. Despite our best efforts we came up with two or three (okay, maybe five or six) instances of a number being called out to me to check off, only to discover it had already been checked off earlier in the day. Oops.

The duplicates were piled up on the ground under the tarp as they turned up and eventually renumbered and loaded. One can only hope that the ones that were previously loaded actually match the descriptions on the inventory (since there was no easy way of knowing *which* box was the "wrong" one).

By the end of the day I was writing numbers in magic marker directly onto the mattresses that were being loaded to protect the van from the side walls of the container. As David pointed out, the mattress is always covered by a sheet—what difference does it make if it has a number indelibly marked on it.

Loading the car was a classic case of *looking* deceptively easy—we had a flat bed wrecker come and load the van onto it. The tow truck then backed right up to the container and the van was backed directly into the container. Surprisingly, though, it then took fully two more hours to actually secure.

I still don't quite understand that, but have to just trust that the truck driver knew what he was doing. He'd even done a good bit of it "off the clock" so that's really hard to complain about. It finally was deemed complete when it was chocked with wood nailed to the floor of the container, front and back of all the tires, mattresses loaded on either side of it, and rope snaked through the wheels and tied off to both sides of the container.

By God if that thing moves at all it'll be amazing. We were instructed to load the car with no more than 1/8 of a tank of gas and I'd been muttering to myself all week that I'd screwed up when I'd filled up earlier in the week. But it worked out almost perfectly so at least we weren't siphoning gas out of the tank at the last minute!

By a bit after 5 o'clock the container was back on the road, our workers had all gone home, and we had Mom and Dad down for a nap (after moving one of the spare mattresses down into their room since we'd stolen their real mattress to load onto the container). I collapsed gratefully onto our bed for a short nap myself.

Actually *our* bed was supposed to have been loaded as well, but there was apparently some slight communication error because the double bed in my office went, instead of the queen from our bedroom. So we would put our bed in the next container and just end up with a spare bed in Costa Rica. A *very* small thing to worry about at that point.

It didn't take long for relief that the first container was loaded to give way to panic that the second one was still ahead of us...and we were a long ways away from being ready. Loading had been planned for Monday, giving us the weekend to finish packing.

But rain was forecast for Monday and our trucker said he'd be happy to come back with the second container on Sunday so we could load then, hopefully before the rain came.

Sounded like a good plan, but after he'd left and we re-grouped from our first container-loading adventure, it fully sank it that we'd just cut our remaining time for packing by half. Uh oh. Maybe not such a good idea, but no changing it now.

Saturday passed in a blur of packing. Looking back it would have been better had we just pulled an all-nighter in order to finish packing, but we crashed around midnight with the naïve belief that we were "close enough" and the loading would go okay.

Sunday morning the trucker appeared with the second container. We had a large loading crew, but with one unfortunate lack—our "grown up" helpers who had been there on Friday had been unable to come again on Sunday. Since our crew had now successfully loaded the first container, we felt they'd be okay on their own for this second container. *We* were there, after all, to be the grown-ups.

But, we grown-ups were still in the house packing. Having not yet solved the universal problem of how to be in two places at the same time, we were mostly *not* out in the container supervising our young, strong, athletic, but not-very-experienced workers. We didn't fully realize the impact of this until many hours into the move when the container was three-quarters loaded.

When the guys carried the first of our stuff out to the container on Sunday morning, it appeared that we really would *not* completely fill the container. One of the key ideas in container loading is that things be packed in *tightly* so that the contents don't shift and items packed "higher up" don't fall down on top of items "lower down" under them.

When it seemed that we would not need the entire volume of the container, we explained the concept clearly to our loaders and had them pack it tightly, but only about four or five feet high, not all the way up. This would have been great, except that—as is often the case—we actually had more stuff than we thought since we were still packing. This is where the youth and inexperience of our loaders came into play. Someone with more familiarity would have likely seen the problem coming, before it was too late to do anything about it.

As it was, the guys came to us after many hours of loading to say, "Uh oh, we're running out of room!" There was less than a quarter of the container remaining—probably only six or eight feet, actually!— when they made this awful pronouncement, and at that point it was too late to do anything about it.

We'd also been at it for *way* more than the allotted three hours, dark was going to be coming on before long, the rain we were loading early to avoid was starting, and frankly we just said, "Screw it, it's just *stuff;* whatever it is we can replace it."

More than four years later we're still regretting things we didn't bring. The entire Part Two of this book will help keep you from suffering the same fate, luckily. Also luckily—for us—we really didn't yet begin to grasp the full extent of what we were leaving behind or the hassles that would be ahead of us as we tried to replace things, so once the doors were closed on the second container, all we felt was relief.

It was Sunday night, and I luckily had enough stuff left in the kitchen (some intentionally, some not) that fixing dinner was no problem. We'd intended to leave a couple of our really ancient TVs behind, along with odds and ends of furniture, so we had a relaxing evening after the stresses of the past several days.

Then it came time to go to bed and after getting my parents settled down in the only remaining bed, we realized that *we* had no place to sleep. (Our actual "plan" was to have two regular double bed mattresses left behind for this very purpose, but one was the bed from my office that had inadvertently been loaded on the first container.)

Hmmm...... time for thinking outside the box. We took the cushions from the outside chaise lounges (that we actually had *not* intended to leave) and dragged them upstairs, plunking them on the floor of my office. We then laid an oriental rug (also that we had *not* intended to leave) on top of them to sort-of hold them together. With a few random linens (that we *had* intended to leave behind) and throw pillows to put under our heads, we were able to make a functional (not to be confused with actually *comfortable*) bed for the night.

I'm not sure the bed would have made a difference. The combination of being over-tired, wired, stressed, and excited was not conducive to sound sleep, so the crazy bed just seemed to fit right in.

After a night of minimal sleep, I got up on Monday morning and went to work! Looking back, of course, this seems ludicrous, but at the time there was no choice. I'd promised to come back in for a final bit of work to "finish up" the transition work for my two biggest clients. (I was a house designer and sales person for a high-end modular home company, and translating my many hours of personal meetings with a couple of clients with complex and highly unusual building plans was no easy matter.)

While it had seemed that I only needed an hour or two to finish up when I'd left work the previous

Thursday, work *always* expands to fill the time available so I was back yet again on Tuesday for a few hours. (After, of course, another restful night's sleep on our chaise lounge cushion/oriental rug/throw pillow "bed" on the floor!)

By Tuesday afternoon, knowing that we were actually leaving in the wee hours of the following morning, we went into full swing on the final moving frenzy. David, to this day, refers to it as akin to the Jews fleeing the Nazis. (No offense to anyone who actually went through that unspeakably horrific time!) For having seemingly packed and shipped all our important worldly possessions in *two* shipping containers, we kept finding things that simply had to be brought with us. Legal papers, files, critical kitchen gear, computer printers, medical items, jewelry, clothes, tools, all kinds of crazy things that somehow had simply *not* made it into the containers.

We knew that additional suitcases could be checked for $100 per bag. We were four people, so that meant eight bags, so we packed up the first couple of "extra" bags without too much angst—what's a couple hundred bucks at a time like this?!?

(Please note that airline regulations have *changed* in the intervening years. Do NOT assume you can arrive at your airport with excess bags. Check first and be very clear on the current regulations!!! I've had clients since then who tried to check even one extra bag and were simply told NO, and they were left sitting on the airport floor trying to weed things out. Never assume. Always check.)

However, as Tuesday afternoon stretched into evening, our couple of extra bags became four, and then six. By now we had used up every suitcase (or vague excuse for a suitcase) in the house. I'd previously bought two sets of nested luggage at our recently opened Target store, planning on checking only the largest, and bringing the smallest as our carry-ons. Ten o'clock Tuesday night found me at the Target yet again, buying still *another* set of luggage for hopefully our final packing.

We'd put a fully-dressed Mom and Dad down around 11 o'clock for a "nap"—knowing we'd be getting them up a few hours later meant we could hardly call it a full night's sleep!—and kept packing. Each suitcase could only weigh 50 pounds, and for years we'd been skeptical about the accuracy of our bathroom scales. This took on new significance now as we adjusted and re-adjusted our bags to stay under the 50 pound limit. Since we couldn't be sure of our weight, we erred on the side of safety and made sure no bag was over about 47 pounds.

By 2:30 am we had done all we could do. By now, if it wasn't packed, it wasn't coming to Costa Rica with us. We had nineteen bags, four animal carriers, and Daddy's rolling walker which would fly for free as part of the airline's "handicap friendly" policies. We collapsed briefly onto the odds and ends of living room furniture and dozed for a few moments, awaiting Jon and Bethany's arrival at 3 am. At that point we felt like we could have slept for a week, but in an extreme version of my typical pre-travel mantra, I kept repeating to myself, "All you have to do is make it onto the plane. You can sleep then."

Famous last words.

— Chapter 7

When we made our plane reservations, travel arrangements for the animals—two dogs and two cats—had been at least as great a priority, if not greater, than the convenience of the humans. We'd often spoken during the summer that we would have moved to Costa Rica right then if it weren't that we couldn't fly the dogs during the heat of the summer. This had begun to drive our timetable of leaving around mid-October—not too hot, not too cold.

We'd spoken with the Delta representatives several times, checking and re-checking that everything was okay with the animals' reservations. We had made plans to arrive at the airport extra-early in order to ensure that they were all "checked in" and counted in the cargo weight so there wouldn't be any chance of them being turned down by arriving too late.

And two days before, after deciding that the crack in our large dog kennel was too big and in too awkward an area to repair, David drove the half-hour up to Augusta to buy a new kennel. He came home with the "extra-large" instead of the large he'd gone to buy, claiming that the large was simply too small for our 85 pound golden retriever.

I had a vague sense that this was not a good idea, but aside from the extra cost I couldn't think of any real reason for the unease so didn't pursue it any further, agreeing that it did *look like* an appropriate size for Hannah.

We arrived at the airport at four in the morning, with our nineteen suitcases, and the dogs on leashes to give them every possible moment of physical freedom before they had to be put into their carriers. (The cats, conversely, had been safely contained in their crates since about 9 o'clock the night before since the prospect of them escaping, thus missing the entire trip, was too real and too horrifying to imagine.)

When we arrived at the Delta counter, we consumed essentially an entire "line" all by ourselves. Between all the suitcases, the animals, Mom and Dad in their wheelchairs, and us, we made quite the entrance. The Delta agent looked up at us and you could see a flicker of dread flash across her features, and virtually hear her thinking *why me, why couldn't they have gone to another agent or maybe another airline?*

I presented the printouts from our e-tickets and all our passports. She had only barely begun clack-clack-clacking on her computer keys and getting us signed in when she peered over the counter, past me, and asked, "Is that an *extra-large* dog crate?"

Something in the tone of her voice made me say, "No, I'm pretty sure it's a *large*." Uh oh, that vague sense of unease about the carrier size was rearing its head again and I was afraid was getting ready to become a lot less vague. She looked at me doubtfully but returned to her click-clacking for a while.

Soon, though, she'd finished round one of the key-tapping and returned to the dog-crate issue. Climbing right over the baggage scales, she emerged from behind her tall counter, tape measure clutched in hand. A few quick measurements and she clambered back over the scales to glare at me and pronounce that it was, indeed, an *extra-large* carrier. And these were not allowed.

They were not only "not allowed" but actually did not *fit* as it turns out. The "commuter jet" we were on from Portland to Atlanta had a cargo door that, plain and simple, was not large enough for the extra-large carrier to fit through. At this news David lost it. (In his very slight defense, we'd now been up for about 36 hours straight and were feeling just a little ragged around the edges.)

To say he spoke *sharply* to the desk agent would be an extraordinary understatement, and it only got worse when a supervisor joined the agent at the counter.

He and David exchanged heated words at ever increasing volume, David claiming it was Delta's obligation to inform us of this ahead of time and the supervisor claiming it was our responsibility to inform ourselves and that this limitation was on their website.

(That vague sense of unease now had an identified root—I suspect I had read this very thing on their site somewhere in the distant past and not paid much attention since, at the time, we already owned a regulation "large" carrier with which we'd flown before.)

But for now I had a larger issue: calm down David, if not the supervisor, and *solve* the problem. Blame, at this juncture, was irrelevant, perhaps worse.

So in my most soothing voice I created a little bubble of communication between just the agent and myself. Angry men on either side of the desk were tuned out as though they didn't exist. I engaged her with my eyes and my voice and said, "Really, how we got here just doesn't matter. We do have a real problem though, so let's see what solution we can find. There must be *some* way to work this out." I not-too-gently shoved David out of the way and, no longer involved in argument, the supervisor drifted away for a while.

I gave the desk agent my look that said, "*Men!*" and we were bonded together in our sane and rational female efforts to solve the problem rather than keep pissing on the tree.

She suggested, "Look, the carrier simply does not fit. End of story. But how 'bout if we book you, your parents, all the bags, and the other three animals. Then your husband can go over to the mall when it opens at 9 and buy a new carrier and we'll book him on the later flight. Sound like a plan?"

Despite the little shock of fear down deep inside me that I was going to have to face this arrival in a foreign country by myself, it did seem like a reasonable approach and at least we were moving in a forward direction. So I gratefully agreed and we forged ahead.

Meanwhile, once David had disengaged from yelling at the supervisor it occurred to him to send out an SOS call to Jonathan and Bethany to return to the airport while we sorted everything out. They weren't yet *too* far up the road toward home, so they turned around as soon as possible and arrived back at the airport, hovering in the background, waiting for further instructions.

The next half hour passed in a haze of more key-clicking and printing and stapling and still more clicking and clacking of computer keys. The tower of nineteen suitcases was providing our agent nearly as much trouble as the over-sized dog crate was. But, bless her heart, she was putting some serious effort into trying to figure out the way to get all the luggage on the flight and with the least possible overage charges. Thankfully—and unbeknownst to us—the "business class" flight we had from Atlanta to San Jose qualified us for *three* free bags each, not just the standard *two.* Clearly a case of be-thankful-for-small-favors!

Meanwhile, since part of that "luggage" was the acceptably-sized dog crate for GrisGris and the two cat carriers, we faced an entirely new animal problem. Apparently there are limits on the numbers of animals that can be carried on any one flight. It's not a simple number limit, but rather varies according to the size of the carrier, so they were calculating if we were over the limit just with the remaining three crates. Complicating the issue was a woman now standing at an adjacent agent who was trying to check in two small dogs.

Although at this moment we were all standing at the counters at the same time, there was little doubt that *we* had actually clearly met the criterion of being there first (having now been in line for nearly an hour) so *she* faced the unpleasant choice of being re-booked on a different flight. (It was *not* a good morning to be a Delta ticket agent.)

For this particular issue, though, unlike the just-plain-too-big dog carrier, there *was* a degree of flexibility. It turns out that the pilot has the option of allowing more animals than the published limit. The pilot, however, typically would not arrive until just before the flight, so the excess animals were in limbo until his arrival.

Lastly—as if she hadn't subjected us to enough animal regulatory challenges—our agent realized that it was about one degree *colder* than the limit for flying animals without an acclimation certificate. I was apparently persuasive in my argument that it was still before dawn and was the coldest the day would be. She reluctantly accepted my insistence that by the time the animals were ready to board it would have warmed up at least one degree and would be okay. *Whew.* Another disaster narrowly averted.

Finally she had the three of us humans, the three animals, and all nineteen items of luggage checked in and she turned her attention to booking David on "the later flight" to San Jose. More clack-clack-clacking was followed by a frown, a "hmmm," and still more clack-clack-clacking. Somehow I did not find all this reassuring.

Sure enough, there was a cause for the frowning and hmmm-ing as she looked up and said, "Well, it appears there *is* no later flight." Uh oh.

At this my composure was in danger of truly collapsing for the first time. It was one thing to contemplate arriving in San Jose and having to wait several hours for David. It was another to have his arrival removed from the equation entirely. I was *not* up to this. I'm sorry. I know I'm a strong, independent woman. I was *not* ready to tackle this move all by myself, even for 24 hours.

As the saying goes, however, desperate measures are born of desperate times. And I was, indeed, desperate. There *must* be a solution we hadn't thought of.

And then, it came to me in a flash. I hesitated only a moment before looking up at the ticket agent and asking in the most sincere voice I could muster, "But, isn't it true that as a service dog Hannah can ride right in the cabin *with* us?"

She, too, hesitated only a moment. "Well, *is* she a service dog?"

We Buddhists believe in something called "Right Speech." In the overwhelming majority of cases this would simply be "the truth," but it also carries with it the idea of speech that serves the highest purpose, chosen with wisdom and compassion. In that moment I felt absolutely clear what "Right Speech" was.

I lied through my teeth.

"Absolutely. I'm so sorry I didn't say so before. See my dad, there, in the wheelchair? He has Parkinson's and she assists him. I'm sorry, we weren't *needing* her for the flight so it didn't occur to us to bring her papers or anything. Gosh. But isn't that true—she can just ride in the cabin with us, yes?"

That poor agent was so desperate to get rid of us, she was as inspired to believe my lie as I was to speak it. "Yes, yes, she can go in the cabin. You just have to be sure she stays in the space in front of your seat. She can't block the aisle."

I was nodding agreement with everything she said, continuing my abject apologies at not bringing "her papers" (not really knowing what such papers would consist of, but suspecting that there was *something* that would officially declare her to be a service dog, were she really to be one), and willing her on with my power of thought.

She happily went about the business of *more* clicking and clacking on her keyboard and pretty soon had produced a boarding pass for David and sent us hurrying towards the gate. We'd spent an hour and a half at this checking in process and now the plane was ready to board.

Meanwhile, almost unnoticed amidst our other angst, the pilot had arrived and declared his willingness to fly with far more than the normal number of animals on board, so the other woman got to fly with *her* dogs and all was turning out right with the world.

At this point my primary fear was that someone would *notice* that there was no way in hell that Hannah was a trained service dog. Hannah's a dear dog, and we love her. But she'll never win awards for superior intellect and to call her *trained* in even the most basic sense is a real stretch of the use of the word. I felt sure that if anyone really took a good look at her they'd *know* she wasn't a service dog. But I sure wasn't going to turn back now. I was going to make her a service dog through sheer willpower!

We said one final goodbye to Jon and Bethany and they carried the offending extra large dog carrier away and we all headed for the elevators. Hannah wagged her tail and did her best imitation of a dog that actually knew how to walk on a leash. Ten minutes later we slunk onto the plane, holding our breath the whole time. But we were on our way, there was no turning back now!

Hannah the service dog and her pal, GrisGris

—Chapter 8

The rest of our trip was comparatively uneventful. Atlanta proved to be somewhat challenging since Delta had *not* (despite assurances to the contrary) actually arranged for a wheelchair to meet us at the plane. Although at this stage Daddy could ordinarily walk reasonably well, at least with a walker or cane, he was completely worn out and discombobulated and truly was not capable of going *anywhere* under his own steam.

Despite his being listed as a "wheelchair passenger" they tried to insist that he would need to board the transport bus (waiting probably 70 feet away from the debarkation point on the plane, where he'd been lowered via some type of lift at our insistence, and then *up* two steps into the bus) but the struggle to walk even a few steps on flat ground proved that that was going to be a ridiculous expectation and we basically "planted him" on the steps of the lift.

We frustratingly waited forever on the tarmac while they supposedly sent a wheelchair. Once it finally arrived (after repeated calls from us), the person delivering it couldn't actually take it *out* onto the tarmac to fetch Daddy since that was a task that apparently belonged to a different union. We finally grabbed it ourselves over the objections of the person who had delivered it to us and rescued Daddy from the glaring blacktop of the tarmac.

Once we finally had him inside, we were able to get a ride on one of the magic super-sized golf carts that schlep folks around (complete, bear in mind, with Hannah the wonder dog on her leash!) and made it to our next flight. Once we boarded that flight, the challenges of getting there were quickly forgotten as my folks settled into their first (and only) first class flight of their lives!

Ironically, in the tighter space of our commuter jet from Maine to Atlanta, Hannah had behaved perfectly, squeezed into the space at our feet. With no wiggle room, she settled down promptly to sleep and was a model "service" dog. In this much more generously-sized first class cabin, we had continual problems with her "oozing" out into the aisle. There was simply too much room, and we spent most of the flight trying to "contain" her in the space at our feet, as was required by airline regulations.

She did, on the other hand, greatly enjoy our lamb lunch, and she happily lapped up her water we offered from our crystal stemware—*after* we had finished using it, of course! Mom and Dad kept wondering if they were supposed to tip, and the several-hour flight passed uneventfully and even pleasantly.

Having learned our lesson in Atlanta, we asked several times during *this* flight to confirm that there would be wheelchairs waiting, and indeed they were. Zipping through the San Jose airport with Mom and Dad in their wheelchairs and Hannah on her leash was actually the only time anyone questioned us about Hannah's presence. We fell right back on the universal solution to many problems, muttering "no hablo español" and ignored the person inquiring, figuring what were they going to do about it now?

One benefit we've discovered of traveling with passengers in wheelchairs is that you now have your own personal "representative" to ease your way through customs and immigration. It's well worth the $10 and $20 bills that end up being sprinkled around liberally!

As I'd mentioned before, a secondary benefit of our hooking up with Nikolai as a driver on our tour several months earlier was that we'd been able to arrange for him to meet us at the airport. Even before we'd fully realized that we'd be arriving with this crazy load of nineteen suitcases, we knew that simply the four adults, Daddy's walker, four animals, four animal kennels, and even a "normal" amount of luggage would strain any normal vehicle. So Nikolai was meeting us with two minibuses which proved to be just right!

We had some anxious moments waiting for GrisGris to be retrieved from baggage (why the cats came out sooner, no one will ever know, but his crate—only slightly larger—seemed to take forever, giving us only a little more stress!) but eventually we had a porter with all nineteen suitcases, the three animal crates (remembering that Hannah, of course, was strutting her stuff *sans crate*), Daddy's walker, two elders in wheelchairs, and the two of us.

Although theoretically all bags are X-rayed as part of their customs processing, I think our tower of the nineteen suitcases with the walker piled on top just overwhelmed them and they waved the skycap through. David was quick to escape the terminal with the luggage and animals, particularly hoping to find the dogs a patch of grass.

The official in charge of animals *did* call me over to his little podium off to the side where I readily handed over all the animals' papers I had been carefully protecting all this while. Of course, it quickly became apparent that I had papers for only *three* animals, but he'd clearly seen *four* animals leave the terminal.

The problem, of course, was that way back when, twelve hours before when we thought David was going to be flying separately with Hannah, I'd pulled Hannah's papers out of the file and had given them to David. Now, however, David had long since fled the terminal, still bearing Hannah's papers inside his jacket pocket.

Uh oh.

Luckily the combination of my *having* the correct papers for the other three animals, my feeble attempts at Spanish (I kept saying, "Mi esposo tiene" which I hoped meant some vaguely intelligible version of "My husband has them"), and my general tiredness, disarray, and amiableness allowed the inspector to feel kindly toward me. He eventually just stamped the papers I *did* have with multiple "thump, thump, thumps" of his official stamps and waved me out the door.

By the time I arrived outside, Nikolai and David had organized our parade. The luggage was in one minibus, with David and the dogs. My parents and I and the cats were in the other minibus, and off we set towards San Ramon. Or, more accurately, off we set in search of a piece of grass for the dogs. At the time I really had no idea where we went, but trusted Nikolai to sort it out and we soon were making a pee/poop stop for *los perros.*

Not quite an hour later, our little caravan pulled off the autopista (the highway) to the steep uphill entrance to "the cabinas" which would be our home for the next seven weeks. These simple little two bedroom cabins were barely finished, but "barely" was good enough, and when we arrived Nikolai unloaded his motley cargo of humans, dogs, cats, suitcases, and we stumbled, shell-shocked, into our new home.

We were met by Adrian Orozco (then-manager of the cabinas), his lovely wife, Ana, and their young daughter, Diana. Adrian spoke far more English than we spoke Spanish and he was to become our trusted friend, our anchor in the occasionally stormy seas ahead. But for now, all we knew is that he welcomed us, explained that the gas for the stove wouldn't be delivered until tomorrow so Ana would cook dinner for us and deliver it to us, and generally made us feel welcome.

Within the hour we were all lying down on our beds, gratefully napping as the afternoon rains pelted the roof overhead.

Ohmigod.

We'd arrived.

Part Two

The Ins and Outs
of Shipping

Some Practical Advice

−Chapter 9

As you've read in previous chapters, when we loaded and shipped our containers for our move to Costa Rica, it was truly a nightmare. We were *not* ready at all. We were woefully unprepared for how to pack and how long it would take to pack. We had no guidance as to things we should plan to bring and no real sense of what would be involved in the actual container loading.

So, could it have been possible for our shipping to have gone more smoothly? Absolutely, had we known then what we know now—which, it must be pointed out, is what *you* will know after reading this book!

The actual process of the shipping went flawlessly—that is, the functional part that Barry (at Ship Costa Rica) handled involving the booking of the container, actual transit, processing through customs, and eventual delivery to our house. On the other hand, all the parts that *we* handled went almost as wrong as they could have since we just didn't know any better. So let's start back at the beginning.

To bring or not to bring, that is the question.

It's almost impossible not to paraphrase Shakespeare's famous line when you're planning your move to Costa Rica. The whole question of bringing your belongings or not is probably one of the most hotly debated among "to-be" expats. And there certainly is no single right answer.

For some people, the idea of starting fresh is attractive. I will say that even *I* indulged in some fantasizing about taking that approach. There are a pretty fair number of folks who recommend this and they make it sound so freeing, so cleansing.

As much as I love all of our "things" I also am drawn at times to the idea of a simpler life. Fewer things to have to keep track of, put somewhere, dust around—not that I really dust all that much, but you get the picture.

But in our case we were bringing my mom and dad (both in their 80s) and felt that it just wasn't fair to them to make them abandon everything that spoke of "home" to them. We'd already eliminated half of their belonging just in moving them from Louisiana to Maine so it seemed too brutal to start talking about leaving behind the other half.

I don't think David shared my even-occasional desire to be free of "things" so it seemed that *our* decision was made without having to give it too much thought. But for many people it is a topic that they spend much more time thinking about, even agonizing over. Perhaps that "fresh start" idea appeals to them.

They also might look at the cost of shipping a 20' or 40' container—which will typically be somewhere between $8- and $12,000, all inclusive—and think, "I could buy all new furniture in Costa Rica for that amount of money." And that's conceivably true, although you could also spend *many* times that amount.

Some things that are locally made are quite reasonably priced, especially some of the Tico wood or bamboo furniture. We have two separate sets of friends here who each had multiple pieces of bamboo furniture made—in one case a love seat, two arm chairs, coffee and end tables, a dining table with six chairs and two nightstands for around $900 (a few years ago) and in the other a similar living room set, dining set, and bar stools for about the same price, including all the cushions for the seats.

And as you can read in all the guide books, Sarchi is noted for its furniture manufacture. In fact, furniture is made in pretty much every town of any size throughout the country, often at prices that will seem very reasonable by U.S. standards.

But many people also find that some local things—particularly the beds and upholstered furniture—are simply not very comfortable. You *can* get true North American furnishings, but imported items here are typically very expensive. There are stores in San Jose that feature U.S. and European brands of furniture but you're looking at prices that will often be close to double what you'd pay for the same thing in the states.

There is a new store right here in San Ramon that sells some attractive and *very* reasonably priced upholstered furniture and they'll even make it to order in one of many colors of microfiber ultrasuede. So there are options if you just *have to* buy a sofa here.

But it's still not true North American quality like we're used to, with a hardwood frame, and serious "structure" inside. It's essentially foam furniture, notwithstanding that it's full-sized, decent-looking foam furniture. And some friends who recently bought a sofa and loveseat there, thinking it seemed reasonably comfortable in the store, discovered—once they had it home and tried to really *live* with it—that it was, in fact, miserably uncomfortable: truly painfully so, in a way that's almost hard to understand.

It seems that the back cushions are so tightly stuffed with little foam chips that they're too hard and put pressure on your back in all sorts of unexpected places. There seems to be a hope of digging into the cushions and removing some stuffing that might help, but so far they just avoid actually sitting on their furniture. Perhaps not the *best* choice! So alternatives here exist, but if you already own good, solid furniture, you simply can't do better than to just bring it.

Local appliances can be bought quite inexpensively. Our kitchen appliances we had in Maine were all at the end of their life cycle and clearly weren't worth bringing. We'd imagined that we might buy things new—with some ideas about buying "floor models" and such to meet the six-month-old criterion to count as "used" (before we knew how little that really mattered!) but as it turned out we hadn't done this by the time we moved.

So once we moved into the rental house we headed to one of the local appliance stores—Gollo, a nationwide chain—and bought a six burner gas stove for about $300 and a medium sized refrigerator for around $600. They've been adequate for our purposes, and I cook *a lot*.

Actually, over time, I've expanded my kitchen appliance collection by buying a second identical stove from a friend who was upgrading when they built their house. This gives me two full-size ovens for the large parties I cook for which makes things so much easier, and still at less investment than a new gas range would be in the states. So I can't say I've been unhappy with that choice. I do lust, though, after a more "heavy-duty" serious stove with enough BTUs to actually *use* more than a couple of those six burners at a time, and will one day order one from the states.

And recently, when another friend was selling their two-year old, 25 cubic foot white GE side-by-side refrigerator because they were switching over to stainless steel, I snapped it up for a very good price. The primary attraction of the new fridge was the icemaker! Call us spoiled, but prior to moving here we hadn't lived without an icemaker for nearly thirty years and we'd really missed it. We've been enjoying our return to that particular gringo appliance and buying it second-hand here meant we paid much less than we would have even back in the states. That's the kind of bargain that can be great when it comes along, but is very hard to *plan* on finding.

When buying new, if you're looking for the brands, styles, or quality you're used to, you'll generally be paying a lot more. You hear a lot about the duty-free shopping down in Golfito, but since we've never done it I can't speak to it directly. I *can* say that there's a lively business here in San Ramon, and probably every other town of any size, of fetching things for people in Golfito.

A number of our friends who were buying new appliances for the houses they were building went this route and to my knowledge are all satisfied with the process. Ask around in town and someone will know someone who will essentially take your order—in our friends' experiences they had to provide a first choice and a couple of back-up options—and your money and make the trip to Golfito, buying the products for you, and deliver them back to you.

In theory you're only allowed one "chit" per person per six months for $500 worth of duty exemption, but as in all countries where graft and corruption are rife, there's a sophisticated system in place of illegally buying other people's allotments to add up to the necessary total.

As a practical note, speaking of appliances, it's a good idea to use a gas range rather than electric. Power outages are not at all uncommon and their impact is vastly minimized if you can still cook your meals. (And as a side note, it's best to have a second propane tank on hand since essentially, by definition, you will run out of gas while cooking. Having a second tank on hand makes this a minor inconvenience, not a major crisis, even if you have company waiting on dinner!)

Be sure that if you have some handy convenience like electronic ignition on your burners of your gas stove, that it *will* work without the electricity. (We have a friend here who did *not* think to check out this particular detail and now owns a lovely gas stove that's just as unusable in a power outage as it would be if it

141

were electric, and that was one of the main reasons she wanted gas! Never assume. Ask. And then ask again.)

At the end of the dry season—when the water that produces much of Costa Rica's electricity is in short supply—we've had days of scheduled rolling blackouts, designed to "spread the pain" somewhat equally around the country. Ironically, the first time this happened to us we were without power for much of the day several days *before* the announced blackouts and then experienced nary a flicker in power during our designated outage times.

And even aside from such extreme and organized gaps in the electrical supply, random power outages occur regularly enough that a gas stove will find a welcome place in your kitchen. If you *are* going to bring appliances from the states, it's important to realize that the gas you'll be using here is bottled propane (not natural gas), normally sold in the twenty pound tanks that you probably associate with an outdoor barbecue grill.

We had several friends who wrestled for weeks, at a huge expense in frustration if not actual money, trying to convert their stoves to work properly with the available gas supply. Certainly if you have fluent Spanish you might find this less daunting that did our friends, but wiser still would be to come prepared with the correct conversion already done to your stove.

Another factor many people forget to look at when they're pondering the question of bringing their belongings or not is that a home is made up of much more than those major pieces of furniture and appliances.

It's not just that wonderfully crafted headboard and footboard that you can buy so reasonably priced in Sarchi, but the mattress itself, the linens, the pillows, the blankets, and the mattress pad (none of which is reasonably priced here, not if you care a bit about quality). And how about towels, bath mats, shower curtains, beach towels, and bathroom scales?

It's not just the dining table, but the dishes, the wine glasses, the unbreakable polycarbonate glasses (remember the tile floors!), the table linens, candlesticks, flower vases, water pitchers, butter dishes, and pepper mill.

It's not just the stove, it's the casserole dishes, the baking sheets, the knives, measuring spoons and cups, strainers, colanders, pots and pans, griddles, and muffin tins. Not to mention the coffee maker, the crock pot (essential for the tough meat), the juicer, and mixer or food processor.

(When our electric knife gave out last year—and call me crazy but we consider one essential for carving the four Thanksgiving turkeys we cook each year—instead of the $10 one I'd accidentally left in the states, we paid over $80 here and that was after an exhaustive search to even *find* one! And it was a terrible piece of junk at that.)

And how about replacing your sports or recreation equipment, your hobby supplies, all the tools in your workshop, your gardening gear, your hoses and rakes, your lawn chairs and gas grill, your weed whacker and books and lamps and TVs?

And while a *few* things are reasonably priced here, most things—if you want standard "U.S. quality"— will cost more, often half again or even twice as much. So by the time you replace *everything* that furnishes and outfits a complete household, you'll spend *way* more than the cost of a container filled with the stuff you already own! (Especially after you have to buy things a second time to replace the cheap stuff you bought the first time.)

Some of these things you have in your home are simply irreplaceable and if you want to have them here you'll *have* to bring them with you. You're likely to want your artwork and photographs, along with the pottery your children made in school and your mother's antique crystal vases. (Bring lots of vases—the flowers are *great* here!)

While you can buy Christmas tree decorations here, are you really ready to get rid of a lifetime's collection? And, yes, they do have Christmas trees here, although if you like a truly traditional North American style tree, you might find that you'll be glad you brought a really good quality artificial tree. During our decades in Maine, we couldn't imagine having an artificial tree, and we did use "local" trees our first two Christmases here in Costa Rica. But when we moved to our current house where the living room ceiling soars to nearly 35 feet, we bought a 12' pre-lit artificial tree and have actually been very happy!

Other things *could* be replaced here but can really begin to add up to much more than the cost of the shipping container. Leave behind the Hoover Windtunnel vacuum cleaner you recently paid under $230 for and you'll spend over $380 to buy the same model here at PriceSmart (after paying the $30 membership fee).

That stainless Frigidaire side-by-side that you paid around $1,700 for not too long ago will cost you over $2,800 to replace here. That large fiberglass ladder you've had for years might look a little ratty, but when you go to replace it you'll be looking at a surprisingly high price here.

And all those Igloo or Coleman coolers you have in your basement may seem unimportant until you realize each one here in Costa Rica will cost $60 to $200+ to replace.

Some clever folks are even finding that it's

worthwhile to spend some time at garage sales and their local Goodwill store in the last months before the move. Some of those harder-to-find items that are so costly here in Costa Rica can be picked up for a song in those places and are legitimately imported as used goods with their low values, resulting in minimal import duties.

Lastly, there's also a subtle issue that some people forget to take into account. Even if you're completely enthusiastic about moving to Costa Rica, it's still a *big* move for most people. The comforting quality of having your new house feel like "home" when everything else around you feels "foreign" shouldn't be underestimated.

So maybe a "fresh start" is the right approach for you. For many people it's not. Be honest with yourself about who you are and how you "relate" to your home. The best advice I can give: be sure you've really thought it through before you get rid of all the "stuff" that makes up your life. Shipping it here might just be the best investment you make when you move.

—Chapter 10

Despite the two containers (and part of a third!) that we used to ship our household goods and car here, there's still so much that we *didn't* bring that we regret. Some things are simply personal and were not a result of any intention to leave them behind, but rather a casualty of our final packing and loading frenzy. Those things truly are irreplaceable so the advice I'd give, looking back on it, is be sure you pack up that stuff first, not last.

A lot of the other stuff we left behind was also unplanned and those things *are* replaceable, but at such a high cost. Other things we didn't know we would miss here and wish we'd stockpiled and brought with us.

So, let's look at some particulars. Obviously your needs are not going to be exactly the same as ours and you might read this list and think "what weirdos!" But consider yourself forewarned and I can almost promise you that you'll be glad you brought everything on the list below (which, incidentally, is in no particular order).

■ **Tools:**

This was an area where I definitely was just plain *wrong* (oh, how David loves to hear that) when I kept insisting that we did not need to schlep the entire contents of David's rather over-stocked workshop to Costa Rica with us. First of all, remember that if you're shipping a full container, weight is not an issue. It's virtually impossible to exceed the weight limit with household goods.

Bring every tool you own. Power tools, hand tools, old tools, new tools. If you don't own a lot of tools, you can't go wrong if you buy up things at garage sales. Good quality *older* tools are often even better than the cheaper new ones. Anything that you don't need you can give away to the Tico friends you'll make and I can promise that your "extras" will be more welcome than you can imagine to almost any Tico you know.

■ **Ladders:**

Here's an item on our "didn't mean to leave it" list that we hadn't realized would be such a big deal. We had several ladders including a 9' fiber-glass stepladder from our sailing days (for use when the boat was in the yard, not at sea of course) and a really long extension ladder.

For reasons that are completely elusive to us looking back on it, we didn't bring any of them and discovered that replacing them here would cost a small fortune. Bring ladders. If you don't have any great ladders, spend the time between now and when you move looking for bargains and acquire some ladders. We have recently begun to see ladders priced more reasonably here and we're guessing that it's something affected perhaps by CAFTA. *But,* I will also say that many seem much more flimsy that you'd like, so I still say bring what you've got from the states.

- **Garden items:**

We brought a reasonable supply of rakes and garden tools, but we sure could have used more. This is a gardening paradise and even if you don't consider yourself much of a gardener now, it's a rare person who doesn't feel the urge to *grow something* here. Things seem to grow as you look at them, so come prepared.

Although you can buy fairly cheap plastic pots everywhere here, if you have some really nice planters—either pottery ones or large fiberglass or plastic ones—I'd have to encourage you to bring them. In addition to sticking stuff in the ground to grow, pots are often a good solution for the large porches and courtyards so if you have them, bring them.

Almost all lawns here are "mowed" with a

string trimmer or "weed whacker" so if you don't have one of these, get one, maybe two. Like almost everything else on this list—if you already have good clippers, large and small, shovels and spades, heavy duty rakes, and compost tumblers BRING THEM. If you don't already have these things, consider acquiring them. Haunt your local garage sales (or tag sale or yard sale, depending on what part of the country you live in) and stock up. Watch for end-of-season markdowns at the stores. When your Aunt Hattie dies and you have the opportunity to get all her gardening gear, go for it.

- **Plastic tubs:**

You know what I mean—those ubiquitous plastic tubs that we all use to store things in these days. Rubbermaid makes dandy ones, although Walmart usually has one of the "lesser" brands like Sterilite on sale at least once a month for $5 or $6 a tub, including lid. Bring lots of them. Pack some of your stuff in them. You probably already have an attic or garage or basement full of them, but if not... you guessed it. Buy some. They cost several times that here and in the land of dampness they can be a godsend.

One additional thought here that I can't personally vouch for—those "space bags" that you see advertised seem like they'd be a good idea.

You know, the big heavy duty, multi-layer plastic cubes and bags that you fill with clothes and bedding and the like, then suck the air out with your vacuum cleaner hose. For extra bedding, clothing you want to keep but don't wear very often, fabric "memorabilia" that you might have, like heirloom quilts or afghans, these could do the trick.

■ **Chaise lounges and cushions:**

Okay, really this probably applies to all your outdoor furniture, but somehow the chaise lounges and all-weather cushions seem the most difficult to replace here. Several times in passing we'd noticed some attractive but very simple wooden "slat-type" adjustable chaises for sale at a furniture store out on the pista (the highway), so we pulled in one day to check the price. When we blanched at the $380 apiece they offered a "discount" bringing them down to something like $340 each.

It made us long for the nice, heavy-duty molded plastic ones we'd bought for some $40 each back in Maine, not to mention the thick tufted waterproof cushions we had. Although we'd bought those in the past at Walmart, and Walmart has a fairly extensive (and growing) presence here, we haven't found anything even remotely comparable. They do have those molded plastic chairs that stack here at a good price, so that doesn't seem to be such a big deal to bring.

But remember that you'll likely be spending lots of time outdoors here, so if you have any outdoor furniture that you like it won't go to waste if you bring it. (If for some freak reason you don't need it, I can almost promise that you'll be able to find someone who does!) And consider bringing (buying, if necessary) lightweight folding chaises to take to the beach. Again, we sure wish we had.

■ **Kitchen stuff:**

Yes, it's a broad category and clearly what seems important to *you* in this regard will have a lot to do with how much you cook, what things you already have and love, and so on. Like so many things, there seem to be two categories of kitchen stuff here. There are quite a lot of things that are readily available and quite inexpensive. I've picked up some odds and ends like small strainers or little glass dishes at remarkably cheap prices.

But most things that come with a cheap price tag also merit the other meaning of "cheap"— they're of very low quality and often don't last long at all. And high quality things will typically be much more expensive that you'd pay in the states. Bring all your small kitchen appliances and—am I starting to sound like a broken record?—shop the sales to acquire things that you don't have or are likely to want to replace within the next year or two.

Even if you don't use a crock-pot or slow cooker now, you'll find one very useful here. Good quality skillets seem to be in short supply. Even at Walmart (called Hipermas here) where I typically bought my non-stick skillets in the states, they just don't have the same heavier duty ones. So here I pay about the same as I paid in the states, but for a much lighter weight, lower-quality skillet.

It works okay but if I'd known I would have brought about six new ones with me packed in amongst my other kitchen stuff, especially since there's some health concern about what happens when your non-stick skillet gets all scratched up and flaky—which it certainly will in time—and you wish you had a new replacement skillet on hand.

Even better than non-stick/Teflon type—at least for your health—is good heavy well-seasoned cast iron. I grew up with cast iron skillets and a big ol' dutch oven, but didn't have any myself until just a few years ago when I both acquired the ones I'd grown up with (when my parents moved in with us) and was the lucky recipient of several more when a friend was closing up his house.

Although I was a slow convert, I can now

confirm that it really is true that well seasoned, they really are quite non-stick, so if you have some, bring them. If you don't have any, you might consider picking up one large, all-purpose cast iron skillet and starting to use it. You can buy them here, but like so many things, lighter weight and lesser quality.

There are lots of fresh oranges, so a citrus juicer is handy. (That I *have* found here at a pretty cheap price that seems to work well, but I still wish I'd brought the one I already had.) Blenders, food processors, toaster ovens, microwaves, coffee makers—they're all available here and will cost you from half again to twice what they do in the states.

And if you want a super-blender like a Vita-Mix or Champ, *definitely* bring that with you. (If you like peanut butter, you'll find that's a *great* use for a super-blender like that—to be able to make your own easily. American-brand peanut butter here is frightfully expensive, and much of what *is* available is also full of practically everything *except* peanuts. We have yet to have found a "natural" brand. Easy enough to make your own, *if* you have a killer blender.)

■ **High quality plastic glasses and dishes:**

Well, you might just consider this a sub-set of the category above, but I think it's worth its own mention. We had a swimming pool in Maine and accordingly I was always on the lookout for good-looking unbreakable glasses and dishes to use pool-side. So we brought what we had but I wish I'd given greater thought to the brutal reality of tile floors. Almost all houses here have tile floors. Everywhere.

So when I found plastic plates at Target in Maine that looked charming and whimsical with their water-colored parrots on them, I wish I'd bought stacks of them. We have some large colorful plastic tumblers that we used by the pool that continue to serve well here, but I would have loved to have brought a few dozen really good looking heavy weight plastic glasses. The ones made of polycarbonate are almost indestructible and look remarkably like glass. It's odd that in a country populated almost completely by tile floors these aren't more readily available.

■ **Coolers/ice chests:**

This is another category that we didn't deliberately "not bring" but it's one we certainly regret. We had several coolers of various sizes including one really large one, several medium "normal" sized ones, and a couple of those handy little guys. Didn't bring any of them. Don't ask me why—I couldn't say. The only ice chest that we *did*

155

end up with here was a very old one with no stopper in the drain that we'd been using to store old family photos.

Faced with the *least expensive* cooler price tag of more than $60 here, we emptied those photos right into a box, carved a wine cork into a drain plug, and returned that cooler into its original usage. We hadn't been able to bring ourselves to pay the price for another one here, so after several years we finally got a visiting friend to buy a cooler for us and bring it on the plane as a piece of luggage.

■ **Linens of all sorts:**

It is rumored that good quality bed and bath linens can be purchased here in select, secret places! They are so select and secret that we've never found them. What *is* available is cheap in quality—low thread count, skimpy, rough—but *not* necessarily cheap in price. So bring several sets of sheets for your bed, and LOTS of towels. Now, admittedly, we use a lot of towels with the dogs and rainy season wet messes, but you can hardly go wrong bringing lots. They don't "go bad" so you can still be using new towels years later if you bring "too many." (This might be an excellent thing to try storing in those vacuum space bags I was mentioning above!)

156

Also, before we came we had found this incredibly soft cozy blanket at a very reasonable price. We ended up buying several since they were so comfy. Now I wish we'd bought even more and just kept 'em tucked away because in time they do wear out—or, as in our case, get torn by marauding dogs. And if you're anywhere in the central valley, unless you keep your house closed up tight (and if you're one of those, why would you want to move to Costa Rica?) you'll find it cool enough at night to enjoy a soft, cozy blanket.

I've also found that I miss being able to buy attractive, reasonably priced table linens here. Again, like many things, even though Walmart is here, they don't seem to have the same merchandise mix at all and I do miss Target, too! So if table linens are one of your things, bring them with you. Don't presume to find them easily here. And even if you don't currently use cloth napkins, you might consider making the switch. The "standard" paper napkin in Costa Rica is a tiny little scrap of thin tissue (somewhat like the little napkins in the lunchroom dispenser when I was in grade school) and although you *can* buy a more substantial paper napkin, it's a good time for cloth!

■ **Upholstered furniture and mattresses:**
This is a "category" of goods that Costa Rica

is notorious for producing "badly." And while taste is certainly a personal matter, and perhaps you will find that you just love the look of typical Costa Rican sofas and chairs, many gringos find that they don't particularly like the styling. And almost all will find them to be uncomfortable: badly shaped, miserably hard, and generally unappealing.

We have many friends here who are very happy with the bamboo furniture they had made with cotton covered foam cushions, and for light use these are fine. But they're not really comfortable and they sure don't lend themselves to serious lounging around, watching TV, reading, and the like. So be honest with yourself about how you live and if you really *use* your sofa or your easy chairs (like we do) you want to bring them with you. Same goes for beds. While it's possible to buy seriously good mattresses here, you'll pay much more than you would "up north" so bring those too.

■   **Fans:**

Yet another item that we left without giving it much thought. We knew it wasn't really *hot* in the central valley, so we very consciously didn't bring our window air conditioner units and we've had no regrets about that. But whatever led us to leave behind our various fans, ranging from little bitty desk models to those lovely new style tower fans that quietly whir away looking a bit like R2D2, I'll never know.

Fans are certainly readily available here, but at about twice the price they were in the states. They also simply don't seem to last very long, suggesting they're cheaply made. If you're going to be living *way* up in the mountains, over 4,500 feet or so, you're likely okay without them. But at that elevation you'll also be downright chilly some of the time, so then I'd be inclined to pack up a couple nifty little ceramic or parabolic heaters instead. You certainly won't need them all the time, but you'll be glad you have them.

■ **Rugs:**

There is essentially no wall-to-wall carpet here, and that's a good thing. I think you'd just be courting disaster with permanently installed fiber of any sort on your floors. On the other hand, for many of us with a gringo esthetic, *some* kind of softness on at least *some* of the floors is a welcome addition to all that tile. So if you have some nice oriental carpets or other area rugs that you like, bring 'em along.

We had a weird little local discount store in Maine that often had very attractive fake orientals for a very reasonable price and in retrospect I wish we'd even bought a couple of those just to have on hand. With area rugs, too, you can always change the look of your home by swapping them around in different rooms, going completely without for a while just for change, and so forth, but you can only do that if you brought them in the first place.

■   **Vacuum cleaner/steam cleaner:**

Of course, any discussion of floor coverings must be followed by a discussion of floor *cleaning*, so trust me when I say bring your vacuum cleaner if you bring rugs. Yes, like everything else they can be bought here and yes, like everything else, they're expensive. Although most Ticos do *not* have a vacuum cleaner (since most don't have rugs) and some Tica housekeepers will be resistant to their use, most will come to love them and if you also have animals, they really are a welcome addition.

We bought a Dyson shortly before we came and are thankful for it just about every day. A shop vac also is a pretty darn handy thing to have and the smallish ones these days are pretty inexpensive at Sears or Home Depot. A steam cleaner is something we didn't have and didn't even think to look for but now wish we did have. Actually, I should clarify that—we *did* have a great little steam cleaning machine for spot treatment of upholstery or carpets and I totally wish we'd brought that.

But in addition to that, now that we're here and living with full-house tile, we find ourselves wishing we had a steam floor cleaner. Regular mopping with the Tico towel mop does a decent job, but an occasional *deep clean* would sure be nice. And, gosh, as long as we're talking about floor cleaning, let me just toss out there the perhaps-new-to-you fact that what we know of as a sponge mop—what I think *most* of us gringos consider a "normal" home mop—does not exist here.

They use an interesting contraption that's a spring loaded clamp thingy screwed into the end of a wooden broom handle that holds a folded towel, or old sweatshirt, or even a specially-designed, store-bought mopping cloth (although I know no one who uses one of the fancy store-bought cloths). It actually works quite well, and they have a technique learned from a lifetime of using this thing for folding and refolding the towel as they work so new, clean surfaces keep popping up.

So it's actually a pretty workable arrangement, but I can tell you that most of us gringos don't seem to be quite as adept at it and if you plan on mopping your own floor and you're used to using a "normal" sponge-mop, go ahead and throw several new ones in the container along with some replacement sponges. You'll be glad you did.

■ **Fireplace/ "wood" stove/logs/alcohol:**

When we were planning our move, David and I used to "argue" about two things—one was having a swimming pool and the other was his desire to bring his old cast iron Franklin fireplace. I would argue against it, pointing out that part of the attraction of Costa Rica was that it was warm and we wouldn't need a fireplace. (Similarly, the crux of the anti-swimming pool argument was that part of the attraction of Costa Rica was that it wasn't hot and we wouldn't need a swimming pool.)

In both cases I was wrong.

If you live in the mountains of the "central valley" at, say, 3000 feet or above, it is in fact cool enough at least occasionally for a fireplace to feel good (and warm enough in the sun to enjoy a swimming pool!) Now, perhaps you haven't been carrying a cast iron fireplace around with you for the past 40 years so this might *not* be an item for you to have to actually pack and bring with you. But I would give it some thought in case it *is* something you want to buy to bring.

We did eventually bring the Franklin fireplace and are currently using it with alcohol fires for a delightful ambiance on cool evenings. I wish we'd known about this ahead of time and we would have invested a couple hundred dollars in some of the remarkably good- looking fake logs made for such a purpose (although you do want to "shop around" since these logs vary a lot in appearance and realism) since they're comparatively heavy to have shipped here through our mailing service.

David keeps threatening that someday we should convert the fireplace to propane and who knows, maybe someday we will. But the alcohol (or alcohol gel) fire is really a dandy solution when, like us, you're not really so high that any serious *heat* is needed. If you find yourself, though, buying/building/living up at 4,000 feet or higher, give some thought to something that will produce a bit of heat when you want it.

■   **Books, DVDs, etc.:**

This is a fairly self-explanatory category. If you like to read, bring lots of books. Yes, you can buy English books here, but it's not so easy. Yes, you can easily order through Amazon and the like, have them sent to your mail-service address, but you'll pay "twice" for them by the time you pay the weight to ship them here. And swapping books with your new gringo friends here becomes a mainstay activity. But you'll get off to the best start if you bring as many books as you can (especially ones you'll read more than once!)

There's tons of DVD rental places here, not to mention bootleg DVDs at practically every street corner, but it's good to have a bit of movie library if you enjoy movies for those rainy days when your satellite TV won't work. For that matter, depending on where you live and your budget, you may find yourself without television, and our friends in that situation watch *lots* of DVDs. Similarly, if you enjoy music, bring your CD collection.

■ **Art, antiques, and the like:**

Another self-explanatory category. You sometimes read advice not to bring your antiques, that the wood will just rot or be eaten by tropical bugs, blah, blah, blah. I would take exception—I would suppose it's theoretically possible to have such problems, and surely living in a non-climate-controlled hut down on the beach or in the rainforest would increase the odds, but frankly most of us *don't* live in that environment.

When we initially pondered whether to bring my mom's grand piano, we assumed that it was folly to even consider it and she—trying to be cooperative—said whatever we decided was fine. So we'd planned to sell it in Maine and buy a good-quality electronic keyboard, but it finally sank in that her father had bought this piano for her and it really held substantial sentimental value. We decided even if it *did* rot away in a decade, she would have enjoyed it during that time and it was worth it.

Now that we're here, the idea that it will rot or be eaten by bugs strikes me as just plain silly. Admittedly, we do have a bit of trouble keeping it fully in tune during the rainy season, but that's largely due to our insistence on keeping our house wide open and unquestionably it's in a "damp" atmosphere. If we kept it in a more normally closed room with a dehumidifier, it would be fine I'm sure. As Mom's Alzheimer's has progressed, she doesn't actually play much anymore, so we collectively value the fresh air more than a perfectly tuned piano.

So to leave behind antiques that you love because you've been told you "can't" bring them is as foolish as my previous concern about the piano. If you really don't want them and want to use this as a good incentive to send them on to another home where they'll be loved, go for it. But if the antiques and art are part of what "defines" your home, bring them along and make your new house feel like home right away, even while the world around you might feel pretty strange!

- **Craft supplies:**

I suspect that most "crafts" that anyone does in the States, people also do here in Costa Rica and there are probably, therefore, stores where you can buy the specialized supplies for your particular crafty fancy. BUT (yes, all capital letters) it could be years before you *find* these specialized supplies, and they're likely to be expensive and very likely *not* of the quality that you're used to. There are no Jo-Ann's and Michael's here! So, if you enjoy knitting or needlepoint, scrapbooking or painting, graphic arts or candy making, *bring a good supply of whatever you use.* You will be glad you did.

While I don't think of myself as being much of a "crafter" per se, I am somewhat of a graphic artist and back in Maine I had an office full of specialty supplies, card stock, and brochure papers. Like many things in our particular chaos of a move, they simply didn't get brought. And while I didn't leave them intentionally, I also had no idea how hard it would be to find anything similar and how much I would long for my stacking plastic chests full of specialty papers.

- **Clothes hangers, ironing board, iron:**

  Like many things on this list, these items are all available here. They're just *way* more expensive, so why not bring them with you?

- **Favorite clothes items/underwear:**

  As part of our last minute container packing and loading craze, I ended up bringing almost none of my wardrobe. In some ways that worked out fine—once I discovered our local Ropa Americana stores. These are a bit like a Goodwill with used clothes (sometimes actually new) normally in very good shape and sold at *extremely* good prices. The Ropa Americana stores are essentially the only place where we—and our fellow gringos—get new clothes, and overall they work fine.

  But if you have some favorite brands or items, best to stock up on those and bring them along. David loves the pants made of lightweight fabric with zip-off legs to convert easily from long pants to shorts and back again and we've not found those here.

  Also underwear seems to be more of a challenge here for gringos. I don't know what it is that Ticos do, but I can say from firsthand experience that you'll be glad if you bring enough underwear to carry you through the first few years.

By the time those are finally wearing out you'll have either found the secret source for a suitable substitute here or you'll have returned north at least once for re-stocking.

In general you won't need to worry about having much in the way of "dressy" clothes, nor are you likely to need a lot of "office" type of clothes, so this is definitely a good time to pare down your wardrobe if you still have a closet full of career clothes. Clothes that just "hang out" for a long time without being worn will almost assuredly acquire mildew and unpleasant smells, so keeping *lots* of clothes you might never wear doesn't make a lot of sense.

On the other hand, I wouldn't get too carried away getting rid of *everything*. In fact, bear in mind that if you have family or friends in cold-weather locales, you might well go back to visit in the winter and when you start packing for your trip north, you're likely to wish that you hadn't been quite so brutal in weeding out your wardrobe.

I've also been glad I brought one dressy pair of floaty "formal" palazzo pants, and I think most men might be glad enough to have a navy blazer and a suit, "just in case." (David has even managed to wear his tails and his tuxedo here, but I'll admit that *most* folks probably won't find a major need for true formal-wear.) Most people *do* find, though, the occasional wedding, funeral, and other affair where they're glad they have something other than their shorts and sandals. In general, though, you'll find this is an informal country as far as wardrobe goes.

■ **Electronics—flat panel TVs and such**

This is more in the "general advice" category than one that comes from personal experience. We brought our 36" old-style television sets because it's what we owned. Yes, they're a hassle to move around since it takes two strong guys and even then it's a little hairy, watching and waiting for them to drop one. Four years later, however, they're actually still working which seems to put us in the minority of *not* having a flat panel TV. But, assuming you're part of the modern age that thinks any TV that's thicker than 6" is an antique, you will want to bring these from the states. *Much* more expensive to buy here. Same goes for your stereo, boom box, computers, weather station, GPS, cordless telephones, and anything else that might pass for "electronics." Bring them.

■ **Dehumidifiers, heated towel racks, heating rods**

Although we find that we generally enjoy the rainy season, "enjoying" it does *not* do away with

169

the reality that Costa Rica, in general, is a *damp* country. Somehow we've had less trouble with this than many of our friends, and ironically I think it's because we leave the house so open. While that could seem counter-intuitive (since leaving the house "open" also allows the moisture in) it seems to balance out since the fresh moving air helps keep mildew and mold from happening.

But almost everyone we know uses a dehumidifier and bringing one with you will let you buy one of better quality for about the same price that you'd get a cheapie (i.e. lower quality) one here.

Our friends, Chris and Louise, swear by their free-standing heated towel racks for pulling the moisture out of your bath towel (which you might find otherwise simply never dries while hanging in the bathroom) if you want to be able to use it more than once. And the heating rods that you often find online for use in boats are great here in closets. (Better still is not to have a closed-up closet, but since that's not always a viable option, bringing a few of these heat rods can be the saving grace for your otherwise damp, musty closet.)

■ **Febreze, food, Sikkens, foam brushes, etc:**

This last category, admittedly a mish-mash of items, covers a bunch of that strange little stuff that just doesn't seem to be available here, at any price. And unquestionably you might find that these items from our list are of no interest at all to you, so feel free to pick and choose or even just plain ignore my advice. But at least you'll be forewarned!

So, for our particular "wish list"—we've found that although most "cleaning" products are available here (albeit expensive) we've never yet found Febreze, the "fabric refresher" in any store, expensive or otherwise. Now, if you don't currently use Febreze, its absence may go unnoted by you. But we find in a land of wet weather, damp dogs, and occasionally musty fabrics, Febreze and its "magic" ability to remove odors from fabric is a godsend.

You're not technically supposed to ship food in your container and we took this very much at face value when we were sent the "instructions" for packing which say that food is forbidden. I've since discovered that we were perhaps the only clients Barry had ever had who actually believed him. Far be it from me to tell you to do something illegal, but I can certainly say that it seems that an awful lot of people tuck a few food items in amongst their pots and pans or bath towels and the overwhelming majority of the time it's just fine!

Canned green (mild) chilies, grits, and good quality brown rice pasta (gluten free) are a few things that simply do not seem to exist in this country, so if those are things that matter to you, you'll likely find that you want to do what you can to bring some with you.

Sikkens is simply a brand of "varnish" (it's not technically varnish but I'll bet you don't really care about that subtle distinction do you?) that we used to use on our boat brightwork. It is amazing but, sadly, does not seem to be available here.

And the rarity of foam paint brushes (again, especially good for varnish) is a complete mystery. They have little foam rollers and things for painting, but the regular cheapie foam brushes that we use by the gazillion on house projects are very hard to find. Buy up bunches and bunches of them and bring them. (Okay, to be strictly accurate, they *do* have foam brushes at EPA, but that's nearly an hour away from us so not super convenient when you want to start a project, so I'm stickin' with my story—bring 'em with you!)

The simple truth is that while more and more stuff is available here in Costa Rica, much of it is still higher priced and lower quality than what we're used to in North America so if you're going to ship a container, and you already own it, and it's useful to you now... go ahead and bring it.

I will close, though, by pointing out a key phrase from just above that you might not have fully noticed: "and it's useful to you now."

For all of my oft-repeated recommendations to "bring things" there is perhaps the risk of my *not* saying often enough, "don't bring all your clutter and junk." This is actually an excellent time to go ahead and throw out those papers you've been storing for decades. Do you have boxes of photographs of people you can't identify any longer? Chipped plates that you've never thrown away because then you'll only have service for seven and not ten, but you won't use them because of the chips? Business papers from the business you closed back in 1998? This is why God made dumpsters.

This is also a good time to tackle one of life's trickiest categories: things you inherited and keep "for sentiment" but have packed away because they're things you'll never use or maybe even don't like.

This a great time to bless others with some of this stuff, or just *be bold* and throw it away. With the rarest of exception, your Tico house will *not* have a basement or attic or many of the other "hidey-holes" that we tend to create in our North American homes for all that excess stuff. I'm all for keeping true keepsakes—especially the kind you can keep *out* in your home on display or use or wear.

But the stuff packed away that you *never* use—you know the stuff I mean!—just bite the bullet and deal with it. Pass things down to the next generation, if that's appropriate. Select a few special items to bring and donate the rest to your local Goodwill or a charity you support. Heck, close your eyes and put it in the dumpster. Whatever. Do you *really* need all those *things* to remember your loved ones by?

We did this somewhat by default when we just got overwhelmed at the end and left a storage unit still partially packed with stuff. I can't really recommend that method, though, since that's also where we left things we *wish* that we'd brought. And some of the excess we *did* bring has made welcome gifts to our Tico friends. But still. Really. This is a good time to find that perfect life balance between "ruthless de-cluttering" and "bringing it all" don't you think?

Ahhh...perfect life balance. It's a goal that brings many of us to Costa Rica in the first place. Might as well start with your *stuff.*

—Chapter 11

Okay, so now you know *what* to bring, and you're wondering about the logistics of packing it all up. When we did this, Barry—as great a resource as he was—sent us an email that, to this day, he thinks is wonderful and explained everything. Ummm, I don't think so. We continued to be puzzled about much of the process right up through *doing* it and learned many of our lessons the hard way.

In fact, it was this one notable gap in the otherwise stellar performance of Ship Costa Rica that led me to team up with Barry (and his then-partner, Ray, who has since retired) to fill in this gap. Barry has many fine qualities, but being a communicator is not one of them. I, on the other hand, would probably slit my wrists if I had to manage the details and logistics of shipping the way he does, and yet "communications" is my *raison d'être.* A perfect partnership. (Okay, perfect is perhaps an overstatement, but it *has* greatly benefited our clients and has given me much excellent practical experience and knowledge which in turn enhances this book. So, if not perfect, at least a win-win.)

The very first thing you need to think about is *what size container do you need?*

As I discuss a bit in Chapter 13, one of the advantages to the great big companies is that they'll come right to your house and do a survey of what you want to ship and tell you what size container you'll need. (They have "industry averages" of dimensions for almost anything you could conceivably want to ship so it becomes a basic matter of arithmetic.) I've also had clients—usually engineering types—who've actually measured their furniture, boxes, and so on to perform a more tedious version of the same exercise.

But let's assume you have neither a commercial mover's estimate for your volume or the patience to calculate it all out precisely. How do *you* know what size container to use?

Absent those measurements, it's an imprecise science, but I can offer up some guidelines. When we were first planning our move, we debated between needing a 40' vs. being able to get by with a 20'. (Although other size containers *do* exist, at a practical level these really are your primary, essentially *only,* size options.) Clearly we were clueless since both of the big guys' estimates came in at *two* 40s.

So one guideline I can offer is simply from our

own experience and now that of years of working with clients. If you have a really full house, three or more bedrooms, maybe a home office, living room, dining room, workshop, outdoor furniture, and so on, there is no way in hell you're fitting in a 20-foot container, and if all those rooms I named are really full, you'll very likely need two containers. (We are *far* from the only folks who have used two containers to ship!)

If you have a "standard" (is there really such a thing?!?) house and you're sending at least two bedrooms, living room, and so on but you don't feel like you really have *that much* stuff, you can probably fit into a 40' container and if you *really* don't have a lot of stuff, you can probably fit into a 40' container *and* include your car. A typical car will take up from 13 to 16 feet in the container, so you're left with twenty to thirty percent more space than what you would have had with just a 20' container for your household goods.

If you aren't sending a car *and* you *really, truly* don't have much stuff—let's say you've downsized already and you're living in a one-bedroom apartment, for example—then you could probably happily fit into a 20' container. But you would be the exception, not the rule.

To help you envision the space in the container, imagine a 10' x 15' room. Go ahead, wander around your house with a measuring tape if you don't already

177

know your room sizes. Odds are very good you have at least *one* room that has dimensions somewhat close—a smallish living room, a largish bedroom, your den, something!—and once you've identified the space, squint your eyes and imagine *everything* you want to take wrapped up, packed up, and piled into that room, floor to ceiling (assuming you have standard height ceilings).

I know this takes some visualizing, and admittedly some folks are better at that than others, but go ahead, start imagining. Most kitchens will take from ten to forty boxes to pack up, a few people only have a handful of boxes of books while people like us had nearly sixty. You know what kind of stuff you have. Imagine the furniture all wrapped and standing on end packed in there, boxes piled up, include the gas grill and outdoor furniture, don't forget the stuff in your basement or workshop... if it's coming to Costa Rica with you, it's going in that imaginary room.

Okay, how does it look in your mind's eye? Your stuff wouldn't come close to filling it? It would be a tight squeeze but you think it would all fit? Absolutely no way, it's laughable to even imagine since your stuff would take at least two rooms that size...or maybe three or four?

A 10' x 15' room holds about the same volume as a 20' container. Once you get a feel for how your stuff would fit—or not!—in that room, you've got a feel for what size container you need. If you think it would fit easily *and* your household matches one of those descriptions I gave above (such as you've downsized and live in a one bedroom apartment), then go ahead and book a twenty. You're probably one of the few that can fit.

Most of the costs of shipping are *nearly* "fixed" so that a 40' container usually costs only slightly more than a 20' container. Although it varies by specific locations, of course, it's pretty common that there's only about $1,000 difference in price. For twice the space, it's almost always a no-brainer to go with the larger size, although clearly if you can truly fit into a twenty, then of course saving a grand is great!

Now that you know what size container you want, what's next?

When it comes to packing and loading a container, there are three general areas that most people want to know about. One is the *inventory*—what does it need to include, how to value things, the format and so on; the second is the *physical packing* of the boxes and how to handle unboxed things like furniture; and finally is the actual *loading* of the container itself.

Here are a few quick facts for easy reference, followed by much more detail for each of those three big categories of information. There's a lot of information here and I can suggest that you'll find that the process is much less overwhelming and confusing if you take the time to really read *all* that follows here. Then in the future you are likely to find the "quick reference" list immediately below to be a good reminder of the key points.

Now, this is also probably a good time to clarify and stress that virtually *all* of what I write here below is relevant to how *we* do it at Ship Costa Rica. I truly believe that this will be applicable as well to almost any shipper you are likely to use. But, of course, if *your* shipper tells you something different, then obviously do what your shipper tells you. Like much of life, there is no single, universally "correct and true" way. My saying one thing and someone else saying something different doesn't necessarily make either of us *wrong.* If your shipper tells you nothing at all on any given point, you will almost assuredly be fine if you follow the advice given here.

QUICK FACTS

1.   It is vital that your *item count* be accurate. An "item" in this case is a box, a plastic tub with lid, a piece of unboxed furniture, a bundle of lawn tools, etc. (You

do *not* need to count the individual items inside a box, just the box itself.)

2.   Your basic inventory should contain three columns—item number, description, and value. Much more to be said about those below.

3.   The list should be one consecutive list of numbers—there's no distinction between boxes and unboxed items (like furniture). At the end of the list please give a piece count—283 items, for example. This is especially important if you ended up skipping some numbers so that the number on your "final" item does *not* match the actual total number of items. (This happens. Very often, in fact.)

4.   You do not need to pack in any special kind of box. Use common sense. More tips and tricks for packing are below.

5.   The container will come to you on the chassis, so it is over 4' off the ground. This is not nearly as much of a problem as people think, but it does need to be taken into consideration. Keep reading for more detail.

6.   If you are loading a car into the container, be sure to read the section on how to do that. It will make

your life much easier. The short answer is you use a flat-bed tow truck to winch your vehicle onto the tow truck, then it backs up to the container and you back the car into the container.

Normally containers are priced for a "live load" where you are given a flat amount of time—usually 3 hours—to load while the driver waits. This is actually very "do-able" *if you are packed and ready.* It *may* be possible to leave the container at your home overnight or even for several days (depending on many variables) which may cost anywhere from very little extra to a lot extra. Barry had never offered this to us since he knew that our location in Maine would fall into the "a lot extra" category. Looking back, though, I think we might have gone for it. It would have cost less than replacing the items that we left behind because we weren't ready and had to load up too quickly. If this is of interest to you, ask your shipper about a "drop and pick."

DETAILS AND MORE DETAILS
Everything you ever wanted to know about packing and loading a shipping container

PREPARING YOUR INVENTORY

Often people worry unnecessarily about the inventory, thinking they have to list every item in every box, and so on. When we were making our plans to move and doing our research, I'd read online of one couple having "counted every spool of thread and piece of silverware" in the boxes they'd packed. Aaarrggh—is that what we needed to do?!?

Since we didn't know (and seemingly couldn't find anyone to ask) when we packed our first boxes— before the George tour and before we'd met Barry—we actually laid everything out on the table and took digital pictures of it before we packed it away, just in case we really would need to have an item-by-item inventory.

Luckily, it's just not that hard. The key issue is

the *count*. Each item you send must have a number and be listed on your inventory. It is *vital* that the number of items in your shipment *match* the number of items on your inventory.

But it's important to understand that when I say "each item" must have a number, I mean each *box*, not each item *in* the box. So each box, each piece of furniture, each bundle of yard tools, must have a number and a *basic description* on the inventory.

The actual final inventory list isn't needed until the end of the day when you load the container, but you'll probably need to send a "sample" before that so that your shipper can be sure you're "on track" with it. The inventory can be in any actual form, but most people make the list on the computer (in Excel, typically, or just a word processing document) and email it after loading. But it can be hand written and faxed, as long as it can be clearly read.

I can recommend that it's actually worth taking a little bit of time before you begin to pack to set up the spreadsheet or other document you'll use, assuming you're going to use the computer and email it. (I also have a wonderful detailed spreadsheet template that a client recently prepared for me and if you email me I'll be happy to send it to you.)

Then, each day as you pack, it's likely that you'll keep some kind of hand-written inventory on a notepad, and if you transfer that day's list to the computer at night you'll stay on top of it and not have a big job at the end. Then you can print out your inventory for actual loading day (in numerical order so it's easy to find the item numbers) and check things off as they disappear into the container.

Your basic inventory needs to have three columns—box/item number, description, value. So it might look like this:

1. used pots and pans, $10

2. used china/dishes, $15

3. used food processor, Cuisinart brand, model XYZ, serial #123456, $20

4. used books, $5

5. used bookcase, $10

6. used sofa, $25

7. used 27" TV, RCA model ABC, serial #98765, $50

8. bundle used garden and lawn tools, $10

9. used bed linens and pottery bowls, $12

10. used lamp, $5

And so on and so on....

Most people will have two to three hundred items in a 40' container by the time it's all said and done.

People often struggle long and hard to "value" their belongings and the best advice I can give is "relax!" At Ship Costa Rica, for instance, we will prepare the list on this end for Costa Rican customs so your list is really for U.S. export, and frankly, the U.S. government just doesn't care that much about the value of a small amount of household goods leaving the country. So my suggestion is to imagine you were having a really serious, get rid of it all *now*, super yard sale. Think of the kinds of prices that would be put on things in that situation and make up your list accordingly.

Ironically people often struggle with this because they want to pay the least tax and therefore have low values on things, and yet no one wants to think that their treasured antiques and art and travel souvenirs and books and furniture and so on is worthless. It just goes against the grain to "de-value" the belongings of a lifetime. Just remember, it's just for U.S. customs for export. Not a big deal. Your shipper will deal with it on this end.

There's no distinction between boxes and loose items as far as listing them. It's just all one list, one set of numbers. Now, it *is* helpful to group things together as much as possible. So maybe your items 1-17 will all be kitchenware, 18-35 will all be books, etc. This is simply because on this end we'll "simplify" your list and put all the "like" items onto one line ("27 boxes of books" for example) so if they're together on your list that just make our job easier. But no one actually manages this completely, so don't stress over it at all.

Notice that everything is marked used. Obviously if you have something that is absolutely undeniably new, just say so. But used is best. A word about this, though—you often read how things have to be at least six months old to be considered used. (In theory that would mean everything newer than that would be considered "new" and would have to have an invoice.) To my knowledge, this actually *is* the law. Like so many, many things here, however, there is a distinct gap between the *letter of the law* and actual practical reality.

And in actual practical reality, this typically doesn't matter. Let's keep in mind we're talking about normal people shipping a normal container that is filled with normal—mostly used—household goods. I'm not at all suggesting that when one is importing a container full of new items that no one pays attention. I'm quite sure they probably do. But for your container of household goods, it's just probably not a big deal whether that fridge is one month old or one year old.

If you have a couple of new items mixed in with all that used stuff, it's not likely to be a big problem, but as with all of your shipping, this is an area to be clear with your shipper about what you're bringing. We recently had a client, for instance, who never even raised the question but simply put *all* new appliances—

unopened, still in their boxes—in the container, right near the doors, so that when the container was opened they just screamed out "New, new, new!!" Not only did this end up costing a bundle in extra duty, but it was so alarming to customs that it precipitated a full-scale inspection. Your shipper can best give you a true and fair quote *and* best streamline the handling of your container only if they really know what you're shipping.

Notice that my sample item #8, above, is a "bundle" of rakes, shovels, etc. all held together with, say, duct tape. No need to itemize as long as it really is "connected" together into a "single unit" in some fashion.

In order to eliminate confusion, if you have a "multi-part" item you might specify that it's combined into one bundle. If you put "item #212, three floor mats" it can raise the question of whether you did, indeed, tape them together into one bundle or if you just unthinkingly gave three loose, individual items only one number because they were the "same" thing, so "*bundle* of three ..." is better. Try to look at your list how someone *else* will see it and just try to make it *clear.* Each thing that has the capacity to be picked up and handled as "an item" needs its own number. It's that simple.

You'll see the major electrical/electronic things are marked with brand, model, and serial number. When we moved, Barry was still saying "anything with a plug" but lamps are an obvious exception to that. No need to search for a non-existent serial or model number on your lamps. Or extension cords. Generally they're looking for that info for electronics, electrical appliances, and the like. And if you've just finished packing your bedroom and now have eight boxes of clothes all sealed up and then realize you packed your clock radio in one without recording the serial number, don't panic and don't unpack all the boxes looking for it. It will be okay. But *try* to capture the make/model/serial numbers for major electrical/electronic items.

And, using my #9 above as an example, if there are clearly different kinds of items in one box, see if you can come up with a single descriptor which would cover them all—a piece of pottery, a book, and a silk wall hanging could well be all labeled as decorations or souvenirs or knick-knacks, for example (something I never would have even said that I *had* until this process, during which time I found that I had *many* boxes of "knick-knacks!") or if really dissimilar, as in my example, just identify the main "categories" as shown.

(Note, *your* shipper may require you to give more breakdown when there are different things combined into a single box; as I said at the beginning, obviously your shipper's advice goes. However, I would limit that to your shipper, not just "advice" from other random people. In fact, a recent client emailed me with all kinds of whacked-out things she'd been told by someone in one of the many online forums that she frequents. Perhaps in someone's world, somewhere, these things were accurate, but for shipping with us, they were not only inaccurate but would have created huge problems had she followed this person's recommendations instead of checking back in with me.

I can assure you that if your shipper has told you *nothing* on a subject, what I'm telling you here will be good advice; but, clearly, you need to follow your shipper's instructions if they differ from mine. They know what will work for the way they handle things!)

You do not need to get into great detail on the inventory. It does not matter whether the box has bed sheets, blankets, dust ruffles, or bedspreads. "Bedding" will do just fine as a description—in Spanish we'll be calling it "ropa de cama" anyway. You might want to put a separate column on your spreadsheet with more detail. You can "hide" this extra column when you send it out to us but then can use when you're unpacking since to you it may very well matter whether that box of bedding has the dust ruffle for the spare bedroom or your own special sheets for your bed.

In fact, this might be a good time to mention that you should presume it will take you some while to get completely unpacked. So you will be very grateful if you take a little time in the *planning and packing phase* to think through the things you will need first when you settle in to your new home. Your own personal needs may make your list different from someone else's, but I can say that *most* people will want to be able to unpack their coffee-maker (or teapot, should you be tea drinkers), a few basic pots and pans, dishes and silverware, linens for the bed and basic bath items.

When we finally took receipt of our goods from the container (having been living in the fully furnished cabina for some weeks) I was so pleased to have been able to locate some basic cookware, plates, and glasses. I'd fixed a simple but nice dinner and we were almost ready to settle down and celebrate our first meal in our new home when I realized that I hadn't actually unearthed any flatware yet. Repeatedly checking the inventory simply didn't yield a box description (even in our "more detail" column) that contained silverware.

We finally ate our meal with the one set of sterling that David (somewhat bizarrely) always keeps in his travel "day-pack" that was a single place setting from his grandmother's silver in a flannel pouch. Mom used the fork and Daddy used the spoon. We found a battered old stainless spoon in the kitchen that one of the workmen had obviously used for his beans and rice at lunch, so I used that and David gallantly speared his dinner with the knife from his place setting of sterling.

It certainly emphasized the point that it would have been worth isolating and identifying those basic things we were going to need first!

Now, *that* advice has somewhat strayed from "preparing your inventory" to discussing "packing" so let's just forge on ahead to that topic, shall we? You can skip to the end of this chapter for a sample first page of a shipping inventory if you still have questions about what it should look like.

PACKING UP

Often folks have questions about "what kind of box is required" and the simple answer is "it doesn't matter!" Any reasonable "box" is just fine, and it doesn't actually have to be a box. Your sole need is to *contain* things and to *protect* things. (Okay, you're right, that's *two* needs.) Where appropriate, containing and protecting can be done in a plastic garbage bag!

I will say, though, that common sense should rule when it comes to boxes. If you have books, you'll be happiest with the smallest U-Haul-type box that's a 12" cube, since boxes that are much bigger simply get too heavy to comfortably handle. In fact, U-Haul actually identifies their box sizes by example of what you might pack in them, and their suggestions are pretty reasonable. (Although they used to call their next larger box—the one *up* from the 12" cube—a book box, which was *not* a good thing. It's too big. But seems like recently they've revised that, so it looks like they wised up on that point.)

We knew someone once who had gotten these gigantic boxes from somewhere that were about 40" square and at least 4' tall. She was so excited about them. Granted, they held a boat-load of stuff, but could barely be handled by humans (they were clearly *meant* to be moved by fork-lift!) and once she got here to Costa Rica, she realized they couldn't be brought *into* her house (wouldn't fit through the doors, of course) and had to be left on her front porch and unloaded bit-by-bit in the days to come. By the time she was retrieving things off the bottom, she was virtually standing on her head, diving down into the box!

Use boxes you can handle. Even if you have movers coming to load your stuff onto the container, and someone will deliver your stuff on this end into your home, at *some* point you will probably need to handle these boxes yourself. At the risk of sounding like a broken record, *use common sense!*

I'd mentioned "plastic tubs" a while back in the

chapter on things to consider bringing and they're great to pack some stuff in. You'll be glad to have some here, they stack easily, they're moisture-proof, they keep out mice and most bugs, what's not to like? Obviously not an economical choice for your *entire* packing, but I'll betcha if you used ten or twelve of them, you wouldn't be sorry.

We ordered a lot of boxes from Uline, who bill themselves as "Shipping Supply Specialists" (see their website at http://www.uline.com) and for exotic sizes and a wide array of materials, I think they're a great source. In the end, though, we also found that our plain old U-Haul store was a perfectly serviceable source.

In our small town in Maine, the "local" U-Haul store was actually a tiny building, barely larger than a walk-in closet, and we routinely would drop in, buy out about half their stock, including *everything* they had in certain sizes, then wait a few days for them to re-stock and go do it all over again. The very embodiment of discretion—or possibly just apathy—we did this many times before they finally *asked* about what in the world we were doing, where were we moving to, and so on.

Plan to spend several hundred dollars on packing materials. I started off trying to keep complete receipts and records, but lost track of it somewhere along the way. I'd go so far as to say we might have spent between $1,000 and $2,000, but admittedly we had more than the average bear in terms of sheer *volume* of stuff and *delicacy* of stuff, so I'll be the first to admit that's probably well above the usual expenditure.

But this is also *not* the place to scrimp. You're spending somewhere around $10-grand to ship your stuff. Don't let it all arrive as rubble because you "saved" a few hundred dollars on packing materials.

The box itself doesn't need any label except the item number (although it *is* a good idea to put a room name on there too.) In fact, learn from the mistake one client made and please DO NOT put the value on the box. It's fine if you want to identify what's in the box although common sense might suggest you not call attention to things of extra value. (I don't think I'd write "silver" on the outside of the box, for example. We don't have a problem with theft, but I can't speak to all shippers' records in this regard and, anyway, why ask for trouble.)

If you've saved the boxes from your electronics, TV, or computer, you can either cut open the box and turn it inside out so it will still accept the ⬜hinking⬜ insets but will be plain cardboard, or use it as is and spray paint "USED" on the sides.

Something that is made up of "multiple parts"—like, say, a sofa and its cushions—needs to be "kept together" somehow to give it just one number. So for this reason as well as protection against dirt and such, I can heartily recommend the "sticks-to-itself" plastic wrap on a spool that you can get... yes, at your local U-Haul store (and probably other places.) Stand the sofa on end, wrap the plastic around it to be sure the cushions don't come loose. Works for lots of things—to keep the doors closed on a cupboard, drawers in a dresser, table leaves together, etc.

If, like us, you own slightly older and already tattered furniture, then the "protection" aspect is less important.   But if you have newer furniture, or expensive leather, or really anything else where additional protection makes sense, well... apply additional protection! Wrap that sofa not *just* in the plastic wrap, but first in a moving blanket. Don't just throw a few layers of plastic wrap around that cabinet to keep the doors closed, but fit pieces of cardboard around it and *then* wrap it up.

Recognize that while everyone who handles your stuff is likely to do so with a reasonable amount of care and precaution (assuming you've chosen a shipper from personal recommendations and good reputation) your "stuff" still has a long journey ahead of it.

First it will be manhandled onto the container and stacked up, the container will then be trucked or railed (or both) to the port where it will be hefted by crane onto a ship. After that a long ocean voyage awaits, with possibly bad weather and rough seas. Once safely in port, there is still another crane trip, another truck passage, and another set of handling as your stuff gets unloaded into the bonded warehouse. *Then* it gets handled yet again as it's loaded onto a truck and delivered to you. Get real. Pack your stuff up carefully and pad and protect it well.

So, you've got it packed up. How do you label it?

There is no official, correct place to put the box number. From a practical standpoint I can suggest writing it on both the top and at least one side to make it easier to find things once you begin unpacking. (Please be sure if you are writing the number in more than one location on the box that you use the *same* number. It is *not* helpful to find a box labeled #122 on the top and #123 on the side!) You don't need fancy labels—a good "Magic Marker" with a nice bold number will work just fine.

For furniture (or other un-boxed items) you can put a sticker with the item number on the back or get some "hang tags" at your local office supply place and tie them on the furniture with the number. If you wrap things in paper or plastic then you can write the number directly on the wrapping.

As mentioned before, don't get too carried away saying what's *in* the box, but certainly labeling the room where it will go is helpful. The idea of consulting your inventory list as each box is unpacked to determine where it should go sounds great in theory but most people find is impractical in reality. (See more on this in the next chapter.)

It is also perhaps worth the reminder that the people unloading your goods into your home will almost assuredly be Spanish speakers, not English. Using the Spanish words for the rooms is not a bad idea (let me know if you need a list) or even just letters or numbers to indicate rooms where you can then post a big "label" on the door or wall of that room. (In this example, "A" might be the master bedroom, "B" another bedroom, "C" the office, etc.) Ironically we didn't do that very effectively when we moved and for each box the guys had to stop and ask me where to put it and since I often didn't have it marked *at all*, I had to guess. Not a fatal problem, but why not make it easier on yourself.

Also, it's good to relate to the fact that this stuff will stay stacked up for a few weeks while in transit. What does this mean to you? Essentially you want to be sure that each box is really *full* to the top. Don't go to the other extreme and have it bulging, of course, but nice and solidly packed.

Otherwise you run the risk that boxes that aren't really full will begin to crush over time, potentially damaging what's inside and at the very least reducing the "structural integrity" of a stack of boxes. Just be sure to fill the last inch or two of the box with fairly densely crumpled paper, or packing peanuts, or even a bath towel—anything that will prevent a "void" at the top of the box.

When we sent our mattresses, we just tossed 'em on the container, packing them around the car as "back-up" padding and that worked fine. But I've had a number of clients react in horror when I suggested that, and I guess if you have a newer mattress, or a very expensive one, you might find you want to take better care of it. You can buy heavy duty bags for your mattress sets that range from about $12 to $20, which can also make it easier to handle them and keep them clean so this isn't a bad idea at all.

If you *don't* want to use your own "real" mattresses as "padding" around the car, you might actually consider buying cheapie used mattresses at garage sales for that purpose. You'll be able to re-sell them or give them away once you get here (to the land of bad mattresses) and they just provide that slight extra assurance that even if your car were to shift, it wouldn't get scraped up.

It's a good idea to wrap your appliances with moving blankets or paper pads and that stretch plastic film to keep them from getting scratched up as they're moved around. If you're bringing your washer, it's best not to use it for those last few days before loading and leave the lid open so it can be thoroughly dried out.

And for your fridge, even though this can be hard assuming you're still "living" in your home right up until moving day, you will be ever so grateful on this end if you clean out the fridge and unplug it a few days *before* you pack it up so that it's clean and dry before you load it up. We didn't bring our big refrigerator, but our small (under counter size) fridges made the trip, and they were hurriedly cleaned out, unplugged, and loaded directly into the container. By the time they reached us weeks later, they were full of mildew, smelly, slimy, and generally nasty. I wish it had occurred to me to let them "dry out" before loading!

LOADING THE CONTAINER

Although we refer to this type of moving as "self load" I would say that people rarely do the physical container loading themselves. (Our dear friends here, Chris and Louise, actually are among the few that loaded their container themselves. They did this in Arizona. In August. Need I say more?!?)

Most people hire a local moving company, some college kids, or their nephew and his friends. Professionals should have a pretty good idea of how to load the container. For the others *you* may find yourself having to direct the process somewhat. There's somewhat of an art to it, but it's not rocket science: heavy stuff on the bottom, lighter stuff on top, packed in **tightly** in order to minimize shifting.

Photos courtesy
Don Clayton

I know that three hours to load *sounds* a little crazy but I can say with some authority that IF YOU ARE READY it is actually very do-able. The key (in case the all capital letters weren't clear) is to be ready.

I cannot emphasize this enough, and part of my emphasis comes from our own painful experiences of *not* being ready. Do not delude yourself—as we did—into thinking it will be okay to be packing up "that last little bit of stuff" on the day of the container loading.

It will take you so much longer than you think, you will pay for hours extra loading time, and it will be so much more of a headache if you are not *totally* ready. Have your inventory list prepared and ready to just check off as you actually *load* things onto the container, have *everything* packed up and ready to load, have things you're *not* taking clearly separated somewhere so your loaders don't have to stop and ask for each item "is this going?" and so on.

As already mentioned, the container is on the chassis so it's a bit over 4' off the ground. People often get all twitchy about this thinking that will be some huge problem, but it's really not. Best is to have at least four guys loading so there's two on the ground and two in the container. Then for something really bulky and/or heavy, all four can get down on the ground and heft it up into the container, then if needed all four can jump up into the container to maneuver it into place. (Six guys is even better!)

For our own personal move, we rented a pick-up truck for loading day to have available as a "mid-point" so we could put things first into the truck and then up

202

into the container. I don't think we ended up using it for anything except our grand piano. But if you're concerned about the height of the container you might find it worth the $60 or $70 rental cost just to have it handy. (Or easier still, obviously, is if you have a friend with a truck.) But it's *really* not a problem to just load up into the container.

I don't usually recommend a *ramp*, just recognizing the mathematical issues at hand. In order for a ramp to go from ground level to the container, 4+ feet off the ground, it would need to be nearly 50' long to have an ideal slope. That's just not practical for most folks, just in terms of available space in front of the container. It also *hugely* increases the actual amount of "walking time" for carrying each box, each item, up into the container. Seems crazy to me.

In the interest of full disclosure, though, I will say that a few people I know *have* rented ramps, or had their loaders bring them, and have been very satisfied. I suspect the incline is far more than the "inch per foot" that would be considered ideal (many times that, it must be), but seemingly they've still found it useful. Suit yourself. Either way will work.

There are usually some tie-down rings or side bar in the container. (The specifics vary a bit between shipping lines.) I would recommend having a goodly amount of light line (rope) available to secure things as you load.

If you are shipping a vehicle of *any kind*—car, truck, motorcycle, scooter, ATV, jet-ski, tractor, anything, large or small—it must have a clear title. If you currently have a loan on your car and will be paying it off before you ship it, *please* talk with your shipper further before you do this.

We've had several instances, for example, of people innocently enough paying off their loan shortly before their planned shipping date only to discover that the title to the car was now off in Never-Never Land and would take weeks to obtain. There are some options, so if this applies to you, *talk to your shipper!*

A car should be loaded into the container *last*, facing out (in other words, backed into the container) so that the VIN could be seen by someone (think U.S. customs), fairly easily. One easy but **very** helpful thing to do is measure your car's length at its longest point and then measure back from the closed door into the container by that amount. Mark it clearly on the container with tape or ribbon or marker so that as you're loading the container you won't have to keep worrying about whether you've left enough room for the vehicle.

Many people worry unnecessarily about getting their car to levitate into the container, but by far the simplest solution is to arrange with a local towing company to bring a flat bed (or sometimes called tilt-bed) tow truck to your home.

One thing to note is that you'll likely face a tiny bit of scheduling challenge with this. Tow trucks are typically called out for jobs *right at that very moment* without warning and often as an emergency, almost by definition. Trying to arrange one *ahead* of time, to come *at* a certain time, can prove difficult. I can only suggest you persevere. Check around with different companies, especially perhaps a small garage or service station near you, where it might be possible to talk with a *real person* and explain the need. It is do-able.

Your car is winched nose first onto the tow truck, which will then back up to the open door of the container. The two will often be almost at exactly the same height. You then back your car off the tow truck directly into the container so that it ends up with its front bumper right out at the end of the container.

You will want to nail a few chunks of wood into the container floor to chock the tires, and it's not a bad idea to save your bed mattresses until the end and pack them around the car on the sides and at the nose as you close the door of the container. (A reminder from my previous suggestion: if you don't want to use your own special, expensive, or otherwise treasured mattresses for this purpose, this is a good time to buy a couple of used mattresses at garage sales. Costa Rican mattresses are generally horrible, so you'll find happy homes for even the oldest North American style mattress once you arrive here.)

Now, as a little added insight into the "nail a few chunks of wood" scenario, I'm going to include here an email excerpt from a recent client and friend. He describes how he'd backed the car into the container up a *ramp* (instead of using the tow truck idea, don't know why) and here's where the fun began:

"Tie down your car? No problem. We'll bring a ramp and you can just back it on and we'll have that puppy secured in no time."

Oh, really?

The ramp shows up, late, and when installed it is at approximately a 60% incline. The rails are about 2" wide.

"We'll spot you so watch your rear view mirrors."

Oh really.

I line up on the rails, Roxann is performing her cheerleader drill (but she flat out refused to wear her cheerleader outfit!) – and "everyone" was seen not at all. Check the mirrors—no signs of life. Turn around and look out the windows—nobody home. Crap. Great.

I can assure you it is very easy to back a car 6' wide into a container 8' wide. One simply closes one's eyes and hits the gas, living with the hope that you'll feel the car go from vertical to horizontal in time to hit the brake and not crush into oblivion all of your earthly possessions. Piece of cake. Getting one's fat ass out the car door is the hard part.

"Out of the way chief, we'll have this secured in no time."

Oh really.

Hour after painful hour passed as we watched the Three Stooges try to chock the tires and tie them down. First they tried screws, but that went sideways when they discovered the cordless drill they brought didn't have the poop to do the job.

"Hey guys, why don't you put down a 2x4 cleat, nail it to the floor and then put down another cleat and nail it to the other?" said I.

Guffaws followed. Followed by the gang running out to Lowe's to pick up some bolts.

Hours followed as they tried to bolt the cleats down.

"Hey guys, why don't you put down a 2x4 cleat, nail it to the floor and then put down another cleat and nail it to the first one?"

Guffaws followed. The gang ran off to Lowe's to pick up nails.

They banged in a cleat and then banged in another and boxed in each tire. Why didn't I think of that? I guess one has to be a moving professional to come up with a specialized technique, eh?

At least it was over. "Did you take the garage door opener out of the car?" "Did you get your handicapped placard out of the car?" Hmmmmmm...

Well, it is over and Rox and I didn't kill each other or anyone else. Sometimes that's the best you can ask for.

Clearly if you're bringing a car, it will serve you well you have some lengths of 2 x 4 handy and some nice large 16p nails. One thing you *do* need to check with your shipper on is what they want you to do with the key. Remember that the car will have to be driven out of the container once it gets to Costa Rica and all hell is going to break loose if they have no readily identifiable way to do that.

In our case (Ship Costa Rica), for example, we often have people actually *tape* the key to the outside of the windshield, on the driver's side of the car. Tape it *securely* so that it won't drop off during transit, obviously. Other possibilities that might be suggested to you are in the car such as under the floor mat or in the ashtray or even just right in the ignition. The problem with *in* the car, of course, is what happens when the car doors are somehow accidentally locked. These things happen. Better to plan ahead and make sure there is a key on the *outside* of the car.

You will need to have minimal gas in the car (around 1/8 of a tank is usually recommended) and most of the time it will be recommended that you disconnect the battery. I have actually read "instructions" that all the fluids should be drained from the car, but that's just craziness since it will be driven out of the container and without its fluids that could be a very bad thing. If you are told this *by your shipper* (as distinct from someone online or otherwise not in an official capacity related to your move) then double-check with them about what will happen on this end.

(I believe that some railroad companies have this "drain all fluids" as part of their standard instruction for transporting any vehicles, which I believe is routinely ignored for good reason. So, not to press on this point *too* hard, but even if you *are* told by your shipper to do this, *press back* a bit about what will happen when the car arrives here. Running a car without oil, for example, is usually considered a serious no-no.)

Now, as a final point, I believe that almost any shipper is going to give you a list of "forbidden" items to put into the container. I know, for instance, our list at Ship Costa Rica says the following are not allowed:

· alcohol or foods (not even pet foods)

· hazardous liquids, thinners, cleaners, etc.

· used propane bar-b-que tank.

· used tires (except, of course, those *attached* to the car)

· used generators

As I touched on before, when we got those instructions from Barry, we took them at face value and didn't include any of the forbidden items (except our used generator, and that's only because we completely forgot that he'd said they weren't allowed) and I've since discovered we're probably the *only* people who took him so seriously. (Hey, after all, it *sounds* like serious business.) And, as I also said before, who am I to suggest you disregard instructions and become an international smuggler. No sir, not me.

I will just, however, acknowledge that this is

surely a good example (among many in this country) of the gap between what is officially correct and what is commonly done. So if any of the things on the forbidden list (either ours or one your shipper supplies) are things you want to bring, I encourage you to talk directly with your shipper and see what they say. You may find that forbidden isn't quite as forbidding as it sounds.

For some people the packing and moving process goes quickly and easily, for others it is a nightmare. The single biggest difference seems to be leaving yourself *enough time* to pack and then to *be ready* for the loading. Proper packing materials can help and hopefully the information in this book will give you a solid feel for what you're doing.

Sample Inventory

Every box, bundle, or loose piece should be numbered and given a value.
Description of appliances, electrical tools, and electronics should have a model
and serial number.
It is best to keep the description as short as possible and to the point.
The following is an example of what it should look like:

Packing list: YOUR NAME
Household goods and personal effects

ITEM	DESCRIPTION	VALUE
1	Clothing	5.00
2	Bundle of garden tools	15.00
3	Books	5.00
4	Kitchen utensils	10.00
5	Plates, dishes	10.00
6	Glasses	5.00
7	Mattress	50.00
8	Box spring	25.00
9	Headboard	25.00
10	Bed parts (bundled)	5.00
11	Refrigerator, GE model #, serial #	125.00
12	Stove, GE model #, serial #	75.00
13	Sofa	50.00
14	Dresser	35.00
15	Night stand	10.00
16	Night stand	10.00
17	Box of hand tools	15.00
18	Circular saw, SKIL model #, serial #	20.00
19	Drill, Makita model #, serial # (boxed)	25.00
20	Christmas decorations	5.00
21	Personal documents	0.00
22	Ornaments, décor	5.00

And so on with simple and concise descriptions and "garage sale" values

—Chapter 12

Okay, you've clanked the padlock shut, the truck driver has secured the container with a customs seal, and all your worldly possession have driven off into the sunset. Now what?

For most people a good night's sleep is in order. Some plan their own travel to Costa Rica for the day after loading but I would discourage this simply because once in a while *things go wrong.* Not often, but it does happen. Let's face it, the best shipping company in the world can't promise that the trucker won't have an accident on his way to your location or forestall hurricanes, blizzards, and washed out bridges, or absolutely, positively promise that there won't be a mix-up with some aspect of the booking, thus causing a delay.

These things don't happen often, obviously, but anyone who tries to 100% assure you they're not possible is simply lying. When you're working with a solid, reputable shipping company, they'll be rare indeed. But if you happen to be the one in a hundred—

or hell, one in a thousand!—that it *does* happen to, you'll sure be glad you hadn't planned the container loading for your very last day prior to flying out to Costa Rica.

So, in general, I would say you want to allow yourself at least a couple of days between the container loading and your plans to fly down to Costa Rica. We had left enough stuff in our own home (some intentionally, some not!) that we were able to "function" for the couple of days after our second container drove away. But, of course, many—probably even most—people are leaving behind an empty house, very possibly even turning it over to the new owners. So most people will need to make plans for the in-between time. A few head off to a local hotel. Many stay with family and friends, some even spending two or three weeks doing "final" visiting before traveling here, which has the added benefit of minimizing the time here in Costa Rica that you're without your stuff.

It's not entirely uncommon for folks to have sold their house and shipped their container here many months before they, themselves, will actually arrive in country. (Typically they've made work commitments they can't just walk out on.) There are certainly storage options here in Costa Rica. Ship Costa Rica, for instance, keeps a warehouse and can store a client's goods after they've been shipped down.

And although nowhere near the ubiquitous presence that they have in the states, there *are* self-storage units here (although do be especially conscious of location if your stuff will be stored during the rainy season and be sure the storage units are high and dry!) and there are plenty of mom-and-pop bodegas around where you can rent storage space.

Most people will arrive in Costa Rica and need to spend at least a *bit* of time here before their stuff arrives. There are lots of "aparthotels" around (hotels that offer efficiency apartments instead of plain bedroom and bath arrangements) and furnished "casitas" and "cabinas"—two Spanish words used somewhat interchangeably for a small house, usually with a tiny but functional kitchen, bedroom(s), and living area. Many of these also offer the benefit of coming complete with owners, landlords, or managers that can offer assistance in all those "just getting settled" activities.

At some point, though, you'll be moving into your own home and your stuff will be delivered to you. Obviously, again, this would be an area where your specific shipper may do things differently than we do, but quite typically your goods will have been unloaded from the container when they went into a bonded warehouse for processing through customs. Once the duty has been paid and they are "released" they would be typically loaded onto a delivery truck and brought to your house.

You'll need to have figured out *directions* to your home to be able to give them to the delivery driver—not as easy as it might sound in a foreign country with no street names—and usually your landlord or the person you bought the house from can help you with this. If they're in Spanish, great, but I know at Ship Costa Rica, and I would think any shipping company, they can certainly be translated without trouble. Just bear in mind, unlike the "normal" use of addresses here which is more formality than anything, in this case you are actually wanting someone to *find* you, so err on the side of thoroughness!

You'll need to be very clear with your shipper what to expect from the deliverymen. Typically they will be happy to spot your furniture (place it where you say) and put boxes into the room you indicate but, again, clarify first with your particular shipper. As mentioned in the "packing and inventory" section previously, it could simplify things if you tape big number or letter "signs" to the rooms and just indicate accordingly. (Then, of course, you *do* have to be sure you know the Spanish words for the relevant numbers or letters of the alphabet, remembering the while the alphabet letter *looks* the same, in nearly all cases the pronunciation is different.) But you need to learn to say your alphabet in Spanish, anyway, so this is a good time to start!

In a perfect world, you would have one person (or even two people!) there at the unloading to check off items as they're delivered. Of course, we know that it rarely seems to be a *perfect* world, so don't panic if you don't manage this. (I will, though, add a little emphasis that it *really* is a great idea so you might start thinking about how you could arrange it.)

Somehow, when we had our two containers delivered, it never even occurred to us to check things off. There were several guys making the delivery and boxes and furniture seemed like they were flying off the delivery truck. I can hardly even imagine trying to slow down the process enough to check items off on our lists, plus we'd been living in the cabinas for weeks with no computer printer, so I don't think I could have figured out how to print the lists. But, *if* I had known it would make sense to do, I could have planned it out ahead of time, had clipboards with two printed lists, and much less chaos after delivery.

At Ship Costa Rica, we've found that almost universally when someone calls up after delivery to say they're missing something, it *is* there, they just haven't found it yet. People have sheepishly called back later to say that they'd forgotten that they'd put a stack of boxes out on the back porch or that the missing stepstool was behind the mattress that was leaning against the wall. Or the treasured sculpture from their daughter that they were *so sure* they'd packed in a box with some other item (which they'd already unpacked and thus were *certain* the sculpture was missing) turned up in its very own box and now they remember thinking it would be more secure that way. And so on—you get the picture.

No matter how helpful this book, *most* people will still find that the process of preparing for a major international move is busy and even a bit stressful. People do things they don't even remember doing—like packing that sculpture in its own box when they were so sure they'd put it together with that other thingy! And if you're not fully prepared (like we weren't) the unloading can be chaotic enough that you'll spend days if not weeks finding everything.

So, best plan—have two lists, enlist the aid of two friends and stress how important it is to check off items as they're brought off the truck, and just *slow down* the process enough to have a bit of control. Note that I mention having friends do this. That's so *you* can still be free to answer questions about where to put stuff and handle the other odd details that inevitably will come up.

Next best plan—after delivery, before you start moving things around and ripping into boxes, go slowly and methodically through the house and mark items off on your list. Don't have a printed list until you find and unpack your printer? The low-tech route will still work fine. Get a pad of paper and a pen and go through each room and simply make a list of every numbered item. You can put it in order later. Start by just capturing all the info before things get moved around any further or unpacked.

Last plan—when you start to think you're missing some things, make a list. You'd be amazed how often people tell us that they're missing some key item, then when they *find it* they forgot that they'd told us it was missing so they don't even let us know. If you want to, go ahead and tell your shipper what you *think* you're missing, but you might use my experience as a guide and be nice and perhaps even *acknowledge* that you realize you'll probably find things but you just wanted to give a bit of "heads up." It's a lot less embarrassing to go back later and confess that you located the "missing" items when you didn't rant and rave and scream the first time around.

If you've packed properly, you should expect minimal damage. I think we had one table leg on a fairly delicate bedside table broken, and the table probably should have been boxed anyway. We had glass broken in about three or four picture frames (out of probably 200 items) and also broke four or five pieces of glassware out of hundreds of pieces.

Frankly, at the time it never occurred to me to try to make those things be the *fault* or *responsibility* of the shipper and I'm still always a bit surprised when people do. Once, for instance, we had clients who freaked out about several pieces of furniture that were scratched after the move, and we agreed to fix them (at a fairly substantial cost to us) although we found out soon thereafter from a neighbor of theirs—who had been there when things were unloaded—that their stuff clearly had *not* been wrapped or protected in any way. We felt a little "used and abused" but honored our commitment to make the repairs, and weren't very surprised to hear in just a few months that these folks returned to the states.

I believe most any reputable shipper will do all they can to take care of problems that they feel that they caused. But your first line of defense against damage is *you.* Pack well, wrap and protect your furniture and appliances, use common sense, and be a little flexible. If you don't have enough flexibility to roll with the punches in your shipping, you're *never* going to be happy in Costa Rica, so you can save yourself a lot of aggravation by just staying home!

—Chapter 13

We've been talking all this time about basically shipping the way *we* did—that is, sending a full container of stuff from your home *up there* to your home *down here* through a company like Ship Costa Rica. Is that the only way to do it? Of course not!

The range of options that you have for shipping will somewhat depend on where you live now, how much stuff you want to ship, your budget, and your comfort level with risk.

If, for instance, you have an almost unlimited budget *and* a very low tolerance for any risk, then you might well find that you'll be happiest shipping with one of the major international shippers like Allied or Atlas Van Lines. These, in fact, were the first people we had contacted in Maine when we were researching our move.

One thing that *had* been very helpful about them is they each had fairly sophisticated ways of walking through our house with a representative while we pointed out things and said *yes, we're taking that, no, not taking that* while they checked stuff off on either a very detailed form or a handheld electronic device. In both cases this allowed them to come back with a pretty accurate sense of how much *volume* our space would take up and therefore what size containers we needed. Like many folks, until that time we were truly clueless.

In both cases, their quotes came back around $26,000 plus duty for the two containers. When we met Barry at Ship Costa Rica (on George Lundquist's tour) and he gave an off-the-cuff general price range of $6-$8,000 for a container, it didn't take a lot of higher math to see that this was a much more economical choice. (Let's remember that was some years ago; it obviously costs more now.) In actual fact, back in 2006, it cost us $15,000 total (including duty and delivery in Costa Rica) to ship two 40' containers. When compared to the big guys' $26,000 quotes—plus duty, which would likely have been $5,000 to $10,000 (more on that later, too)—it was a real no-brainer for us.

BUT, it's not a 100% apples-to-apples comparison. For their *much* higher price they would have come in and packed and wrapped everything for us, they would have professionally loaded the containers, and they would have fully insured everything. So, back to my original statement—if you have a generous budget and a low risk-tolerance, they could actually be a valid choice.

For others, more like us, on a tighter budget and willing to do more of the work ourselves, an agent like

Ship Costa Rica was by far a better choice. There are certainly other companies that act in a similar manner and getting recommendations from people who have actually successfully used them for shipping is probably your single best resource. We were so pleased with Ship Costa Rica, for instance that I eventually teamed up with Barry, so clearly the things I know about first hand have to do with that company. But it would be disingenuous of me to suggest that there are no other decent shippers out there, so, again, recommendations are a great way to go.

I spoke of "risk tolerance" when talking about using one of the "big guys" and you may wonder what risks I'm referring to. One is that you will *not* likely be able to get "scratch and dent" insurance for your shipment since you have packed it yourself. Understandably, companies aren't interested in insuring against breakage or damage on a PBO (packed by owner) shipment since there's no way at all to determine whether you did a good job of wrapping, packing, and protecting your goods or not.

Your single biggest "insurance" is, in fact, the reputation of the company shipping you and the thoroughness with which you properly prepare your boxes and furniture for shipment. That's largely what this whole second section of this book deals with, so you should be in good shape after reading this. But, of course, even then you have to actually *put into practice* what you read about!

What if, despite reading my recommendations to *bring your stuff*, you really have nowhere near a container-load to bring? You'll still have options, although of course they'll typically cost more on a "cubic foot" basis than sending a full container. On the other hand, a full container that actually only has a small amount of stuff in it isn't very economical either, so options are good.

It's surprisingly difficult to find out just what those might be, actually, and frankly I don't pretend to give an encyclopedic rundown on them here. But here's a bit of example of the *kinds* of possibilities there are.

One is simply that your shipper might be able to pair you up with someone else nearby who is shipping at the same time and who would have room to spare— thus room to share!—in their container. This is usually considerably more work for the shipper and many of the costs are actually duplicated rather than being halved, so most shippers will charge each party more than simply taking *one* container price and pro-rating it straight line to the two people. But, even so, if it happens to work out, it can be a viable alternative and cost-savings.

A slight variation on that theme is that you, yourself, find someone with whom to share. The online boards and forums can be a resource to find a container-mate, or perhaps you're actually making plans with other friends or family members to move together. Again, you should expect that the container is likely to cost somewhat more than if there were simply one household in it, but should still produce a good savings for you.

This approach can be helpful if you're *really* not shipping much stuff, since *many* people moving are likely to have space for your twelve boxes of treasures, *or* if you actually have something that's nearly enough for a 20' container and can find someone else with a similar amount of stuff since splitting a 40' container (even with the "sharing premium" on the price) is a good bit less than paying for a 20-footer.

But, let's face it, North America is a *big* place, and the odds of finding someone else moving from very nearby at the precise same time you are and with just the right "volume" of stuff to pair with yours... well, it's not really all that common for that to work out. It *could*, but as the saying goes, I wouldn't hold your breath.

So...other options? Many of the shippers to Costa Rica have various services for less than container load (LCL) shipping. So first recommendation is simply to ask yours! Unlike a container which will be brought right to your home, LCL shipping is done usually from one or more major ports—often Los Angeles, Tampa or Miami, and maybe somewhere on the northeast coast like New York or New Jersey. So you might have to get your stuff from your house to their warehouse in one of those cities but, again, if you ask your shipper, they're pretty likely to be able to point you in the right direction. For example, FedEx has a "freight" division that is much less expensive than you might imagine.

Another option for small amounts of stuff is CargaTica. They're a freight consolidator with offices in Alajuela and the Miami area. I have friends here in Costa Rica who have used them quite happily. They do have someone in Alajuela who can process your things through customs, as I understand it, for an extra fee, or you can tackle it yourself. (Not me, thank you very much.) In Miami you can call them at 305.477.5508 or 506.2443.7058 in Alajuela. Also, check out their website at http://www.cargatica.com for more info. I can't speak to it personally, but I've heard enough good things to feel confident suggesting they're at least a worthwhile option to investigate.

And, perhaps lastly, there's the option that you'll often hear about, which is simply to pay the "excess luggage" charges and bring extra suitcases, boxes, or plastic tubs on the plane with you. Often folks of the "start fresh" mentality are practically militant about suggesting that this is the *only* way to bring your small amount of personal treasures to Costa Rica. As you've read, we somewhat took this route (despite the seeming abundance of shipping space we had in two 40' containers) simply because we ended up with too many things left over that we felt we simply *had to* bring.

Unfortunately, just like with our nineteen suitcases, often those people most vigorously suggesting you just bring your stuff in extra suitcases did it some years in the *past*. Since most airlines have put much more stringent baggage restrictions in place in the past year or two, please do not *assume* that this will be a viable option until you've checked (and then double-checked) with your airline. Not just *any* airline, but the specific airline you will be flying.

I've known several people who actually arrived at the airport with their extra bags, only to be told that it wasn't a matter of just "paying extra" but that extra bags simply weren't allowed. For any price!

Oops.

Imagine sitting on the airport floor trying to compress three suitcases into two, trying to decide what to leave behind, especially when you might or might not even have someone there with you who can take things back home for you to be able to collect somehow in the future.

It's not a pretty picture.

So, if you want to try this approach, I can only re-emphasize the recommendation to talk with your airline. Be clear about the dates you'll be traveling—there are much more restrictive limitations, for instance, during certain holiday periods—and it wouldn't hurt to call a couple of times and talk with different folks to *be sure!*

In general, most airlines charge something on the order of $100 per extra bag, and the typical large suitcase holds around three-and-a-half cubic feet. (Since the airlines charge by "total inches" of length+width+height instead of cubic feet, they're not directly "transferable" concepts, but your typical "biggest size allowed" suitcase does, in fact, hold about 3.6 cubic feet. Mas o menos.) So, call it $25 a cubic foot with most likely nothing extra for duty, it's not a terrible way to go if you *really* only have a few extra bags. Again (hmmm, I'd think I was sounding like a broken record if it weren't so important!) check with your airline.

So, there you have it...you've read how we decided to move to Costa Rica and how we did it, you've read some very specific advice on the logistics, and seen a few of the options for how to get your stuff down here. There's much more information coming in the rest of the book series, but I'm going to get things started with a third section of *this* book, cleverly named "More Useful Stuff" which follows right here.

Unlike many "appendices" that are of interest only to a very few people looking for facts, figures, and formulas, the "Part Three" of this book actually *does* contain a heck of a lot of useful information that simply didn't *fit* elsewhere within the flow of the book. I encourage you to read on. Particularly the next-to-last chapter, "Reality Check." And if *your* "Reality Check" confirms that you think this is a move you want to make, we look forward to meeting you someday.

Part Three

More Useful Stuff!

—Research and Resources

In Chapter 2, I spoke briefly of my "research" phase, searching online and reading books to see if this was an idea that had any merit. Here, in hopes it might provide you with some useful "direction" in your own research, I've given a bit more of the nitty-gritty detail.

The first starting point for me—and perhaps for most folks these days—was the internet. Type "retiring to Costa Rica" into Google and you'll get well over 6,000,000 results. Using the more generic term "moving" (instead of retiring) and that goes up to 13,000,000 results. Even discounting 95% of those as potentially irrelevant, that still leaves lots of possible websites to look at. One by one I unearthed sites where I could read about the country, its history and politics, its attitude toward North Americans, its climate, medical services, and education.

Helpful background, but one of the hardest things at that point was to find "real" people who had done what we were considering doing. Everywhere I looked I *read* that the gringos had moved to the country en masse, but finding any to actually *talk* to was hard.

So initially I settled for gathering as much "factual" information as I could. I found sites such as the recently launched (back then) "Real Costa Rica" (http://www.therealcostarica.com) and Scott Oliver's "We Love Costa Rica" (http://www.welovecostarica.com) which both have lots of articles.

I did notice—even then, and I think it's only gotten worse over the years—that there seemed to be a lot of "backbiting" between the different sites, each alluding to the perceived failings of the others. (I'm not speaking specifically about those two named, rather between practically all site owners, tour operators, authors, and so on.)

And it *is* true, now that I'm here and have much more knowledge of my own, I can see that there are errors, inconsistencies, or just plain "distorted orientations" of virtually all the sites, but even so I say don't throw the baby out with the bathwater. They're all useful at this phase of intense information gathering—just keep that healthy skepticism in place and don't take any single thing you read as the absolute gospel.

(And, sure, this applies to me, too! I think I'm better than many are at being "objective" and presenting all sides of something, but even so all I can do is share with you "my" truth, as I know it. So if you have an experience or "know" something different than I say, well, more power to you. It's all about finding what's "true" for you! I'm sure gonna do my best to tell you what's true as I know it.)

Medical care was a key concern—with my dad's Parkinson's, my mom's dementia and celiac/sprue disease, and David's multitude of conditions including high blood pressure, prostate problems, ADD, depression, spinal stenosis, and chronic nerve pain (wow, when you put it like that it's hard to believe he's walking around seeming pretty "normal" huh?!?) we were on the lookout for information that would confirm that they'd all be able to get (and afford) the care—including medications—that they needed.

I discovered the world of forums such as http://groups.yahoo.com/group/CostaRicaLiving (the Yahoo Group, "Costa Rica Living" commonly referred to as CRL), and the forum at We Love Costa Rica (http://www.welovecostarica.com) and at the ARCR, the Association of Residents of Costa Rica (http://www.arcr.net) and spent hours poring through the archives.

Almost any topic conceivable has been covered—sometimes ad nauseam—over the years on the forums, and certainly I was able to find enough references to people's medical experiences to reassure us that we weren't insane to be considering this move. [I speak in much more depth about our medical experiences in *Living (and Dying) in Costa Rica, A Health and Medical*

Perspective, another book in this series, due to be published soon and also in "Reality Check" here later in this book.]

There's a lot of good information to be found in all of the forums, although like all things internet, it's wise to keep that virtual salt-shaker handy and take the advice with the proverbial grain of salt. In time you'll learn which people tend to have good advice, which ones just like to complain, who is really looking to be helpful vs. who just likes to snipe at others.

But at first, just take it all in and recognize that while anything and everything posted might be "true" for the person posting it, that is not to be mistaken for "truth" in the larger sense of the word. Be open-minded and be a skeptic at the same time. Like much of life, it requires a balance!

When we were researching, I wanted real people to talk to, but I didn't know any. I discovered that folks often created *different* screen names at the different sites, and while many sites *don't* publish the poster's email address, the yahoo groups *do*—although only if you get the daily digest version, a little "inside trick" that I stumbled onto completely serendipitously.

So, I found that if I paid close enough attention as I read the different forums, I could sometimes eventually match up a screen name from one site to a "real name" (or, at least, real email address) on another site. I felt like a stalker as I would track postings to see if I could turn these usually anonymous tidbits into real people.

And when I did, halleluiah, I emailed them and found everyone to be kind and willing to answer questions. One of the problems, I found though, is that I often simply didn't even know the questions to ask. One of my favorite lines is "you don't know what you don't know" and it sure seems to apply to this process! (One of my goals for these books, in fact, is to help answer the questions *you* don't know to ask, too!)

The world of blogging was still quite new then, and it took me many months to even discover it existed, much less find useful blogs. But I felt like I'd found the motherlode when I stumbled across Jen Sheridan's blog "A New Life In Costa Rica" (http://www.anewlifeincostarica.com) since they lived (still live) right in San Ramon which was a town we'd begun to zero in on.

At that time they had only recently moved to Costa Rica themselves, so her blog was full of useful insights as they went through the very process that we were planning. If you're researching and planning a move, be sure to go back to her earliest posts since they're likely to be most helpful.

And Sally O'Boyle's "A Broad in Costa Rica" is something I still enjoy reading today, several years after

I first found it and started mining its posts for useful information. (http://www.abroadincostarica.com) Sally is an insightful and funny writer and life observer, and her blog has continued to hold my interest over the years but, again, for your initial research, there's value in digging back into the archives for her early days. Sally, interestingly enough, has at time of this writing actually moved back to the states after almost five years here. But that doesn't negate in any way the usefulness of her blog for research!

Both Jen and Sally keep a pretty current list of other interesting blogs on their sites, too, so there's a wealth of personal stories out there now. But it's important to recognize that blogging in general is simply people rambling online about their daily experiences.

Their actual usefulness to you in your research will vary and most do *not* consider it their responsibility to educate you about what to expect when you move. They're just thinking' out loud, so to speak, and some have much more useful thoughts than others.

Some just like to piss and moan and bitch about things, some have a particular interest or orientation that you might find either fascinating or mind-numbingly boring, so look around, pick and choose, and take from them what seems useful to you.

A couple of new sites that friends who recently moved here keep are "Retire for Less in Costa Rica" (http://www.retireforlessincostarica.com), a blog that Paul and Gloria Yeatman keep and "Boomers Offshore" (http://www.boomersoffshore.com) which uses mostly video to document Fran and Andy Browne's move here. Both couples are recent transplants so they both give some great insight into the real process of some real people.

Moving along from the informational sites and personal blogs, there are two well-recognized online English daily "newspapers" that you might find interesting: A.M. Costa Rica (http://www.amcostarica.com) and Inside Costa Rica (http://www.insidecostarica.com) and if you're a fan of daily news, you can certainly at least see what's being talked about here.

Bridging the virtual and paper-and-ink worlds is the English language newspaper, The Tico Times, published weekly. It's available online at http://ticotimes.net —notice the dot-net ending, quite essential to actually being at the website of the newspaper, although the dot-com domain is a web site that has a number of interesting articles about Costa Rica. Just remember the Ns—"net for newspaper" at least in this particular case.

Reading *The Tico Times* is another case of needing to maintain your sense of intelligent "filtering" in place. We subscribed to the paper while still in the states, first online and then receiving the mailed copy— yes, it comes to you a couple of weeks late, but that's rarely a major problem, especially when reading from afar—and David still buys a copy religiously each week. I've become sufficiently jaded about its accuracy that I'm less of a fan, but as David pointed out one day recently, I should perhaps apply my "don't throw the baby out with the bathwater" rule here and be less critical.

Like all the resources I mention here, I *will* say that it's worth reading, especially in this research phase. You *must* be aware, though, that we frequently find "facts" that seem so completely absurd that they couldn't possibly have passed by any serious editorial review, so when you read something that seems like it just couldn't be true, there's a *chance* it simply might not be.

Although the internet held a wealth of information when were researching, we still found that the basic "moving to Costa Rica" books were invaluable as well. As I mentioned before, we didn't buy a single "tour" book or travel guide about Costa Rica until long after we lived here and then bought a couple to have available for visitors, but we did find several broad-based books about living here and we bought and devoured those.

Erin Van Rheenen's *Living Abroad in Costa Rica* was one of the first ones we bought, and even now years later it can be interesting to read back through some of it. At the time we were initially researching I had to be careful to buy at least two books at a time (for instance this one and John Howells' *Choose Costa Rica for Retirement*) so that David and I didn't have to fight over having a "Costa Rica" book to read!

Erin's book was re-issued and presumably updated in 2007 and put out under the "Moon" umbrella. I always find it useful to look over the reader's reviews on Amazon, and the reviews for *Living Abroad* are almost universally very good.

Ironically, one of the few complaints reviewers make is that she isn't *really* a resident of Costa Rica, and I had come away with that suspicion, too, when reading the book which put me off of it a bit. It does appear that however she does it, though, she does a good job of updating and the book is well written, so that's a slightly specious argument—if the book is accurate it shouldn't really matter *where* she lives.

Choose Costa Rica for Retirement similarly covers a broad spectrum of information about moving to Costa Rica and does it well. Like Erin's book, this one is periodically updated and Amazon shows that the most recent is the 9th edition (two editions newer my 7th) published in 2008. One personal observation is that Howells' book, unfortunately, is typeset in a very delicate sans-serif typeface that's pretty, but somewhat difficult to read, especially ironic when you consider that by definition (given its name) it is oriented to a slightly aging reader!

Christopher Howard's book, *The New Golden Door to Retirement and Living in Costa Rica*, was physically frustrating to read because it was full of typos and the binding fell apart almost immediately, but similarly had lots of information in it that we found useful in our initial research. Howard's book is full of "recommendations" for professionals in many different areas. Some readers find these recommendations invaluable, others see them simply as advertisements and find them obnoxious and pushy. Consider yourself forewarned. They didn't particularly bother me.

One of the biggest issues is that things *change* pretty frequently, so requirements for residency, for bringing in pets, traffic laws, attitudes toward enforcing laws, and certainly costs for things change so quickly that published hard copy "reference" books like these are often outdated in at least *some* area practically as soon as they're published.

And, in fact, although part of the beauty of the internet is that it can be updated so much more easily than a hard-copy book, many web sites are also way behind in their facts and figures. So it's wise to take *all* data you read with an open mind and an acknowledgement that important facts should be checked with the appropriate current authority. Notwithstanding that, though, I'd still strongly suggest they're all well worth reading.

The single biggest problem with most of the books—from *my* perspective—is that they're *too* complete. Obviously a somewhat strange complaint, since they can hardly be faulted for being thorough, but in trying to be everything to everybody, they didn't give me the thing I craved the most, which was a sense of *someone real*, someone *like us,* who had made the move somewhat recently and could really speak to it in detail. So my search continued.

Another form of "research" that we initially rejected and ultimately became the smartest thing we ever did, is the "move to Costa Rica" tour. There are a number available and they differ quite dramatically from your classic "tourist" tour. These tours are *not* about seeing the sights. Don't expect lazy days on the beaches or exhilarating treks through the jungle or dramatic views of volcanoes spewing molten lava.

These tours are designed—in theory at least—to give you insight into what it's like to *move* to Costa Rica, to *live* in Costa Rica, to build or buy a house in

Costa Rica, and so on. As more and more folks investigate coming to Costa Rica, more and more tours are popping up. I won't even try to address anything beyond what I consider to be the big three. Of those three, we ended up taking *one* which I can enthusiastically recommend. The others? Well, read on.

At the time we were investigating, the big three were only the big two. One was Christopher Howard's tour, which you frequently read about and see advertised. As mentioned above, he is the author of one of the guidebooks to moving here and is undoubtedly seen as an authority. I actually have no facts to dispute that claim, nor do I wish to try.

I *can* speak, though, to *value*, and for that we'll just do a quick run-down on the price. Although his regular price (at time of this writing) is $1,349 per person, he seems to regularly run a special of $1,049 per person for a couple. (A single pays a slight premium of $1,199 per person.) So for simple math let's take a typical couple who buys now on the sale price, who will be handing over $2,098 for a tour showing, at first glance, a 6-day itinerary. Okay, doesn't sound too bad.

But when you look a bit closer at the itinerary, you see that day one is your arrival where the tour "activity" consists of picking you up at the airport and taking you to the hotel. (And, yes, you paid your own airfare of course.) And day 6 is departure day, so again the only tour activity is your trip to the airport—although if you have any sense you won't leave then, but stay on to further explore based on what you learned from the tour. So, for our money, we're now down to 4 days where the itinerary actually indicates a real activity.

Ahh, but further inspection reveals that the first two days are, in fact, attendance at the ARCR (Association of Residents of Costa Rica) seminar, which you could attend on your own for only $65—or only $40 if you're an ARCR member.

So now you're basically down to two days of actual "touring" on this tour, on days "4 and 5" of the itinerary. Over two grand (nearly $2,700 when he's not running his "special") for a couple, and you got 5 nights of hotel—and certainly $50 a night will buy you many a nice hotel room in the central valley so let's say a $250 value, $130 worth of ARCR seminar for two, 4 days of meals—so being generous we'll say $200 for that, and 2 days of actual touring. You do the math.

So, even before we knew enough to fully understand what "value" or not was inherent in Christopher Howard's tour, we knew that it simply wasn't within our budget. In fact, even George Lundquist's tour "Retire on Social Security" (http://www.costaricaretireonss.com) initially seemed high to us, just because we were on such a tight budget and knew that we could pay for hotel rooms and meals for less money.

But George wisely charges only slightly more for a couple than for a single (rather than a "per person" price for both people) which covers the actual additional food cost. So his tour, even in just simple dollars, is a much more reasonable $1,190 total for two people.

And in "value" for that money, I can hardly even say enough to adequately convey what great value we got.

So how did we end up on his tour since we'd initially ruled it out? As we tried to make plans for our one-and-only scouting mission to Costa Rica, we were dependent on my brother being able to come to Maine from Philadelphia to stay with Mom and Dad. When dates finally became clear for that and we started to finalize our own plans, someone posted a glowing recommendation for George's tour on the Costa Rica Living [Yahoo] group.

I went to his website again—having looked at it briefly in the past—and saw that he had a tour starting two days after the date we were now planning on arriving in Costa Rica. That seemed a bit like destiny and as we calculated costs again (including the realization that we would have had to rent a car for those same days if we were just looking around on our own) we suddenly understood that his tour was looking more and more like a bargain. I wrote in depth in Chapter 3 about our actual experiences on that trip.

In closing this overview of the tours, let me add one last bit about a slightly "newer" presence on the tour scene, one I'm now including in my "big three." Based right here in San Ramon is the Boomers in Costa Rica tour (http://boomersincostarica.com) led by Andrew Mastrandonas. As the name would suggest, he's targeting a slightly younger audience (no mention of social security here!) although in practical reality I think both his and George's tour get a similarly mixed age group.

Since we haven't taken his tour I can't say anything about it firsthand, but we have good friends here who *did* take it and speak highly of it. I will say that I'm pretty sure they give good value, and are priced just a bit more than George's (currently the Boomers price is $1,499 for a couple or $1,299 a single) so he, too, follows the very sane approach of only charging a bit extra for the second person.

So, I feel like you can't really go wrong with either Andrew's or George's tour. As I've said before, we sure are thankful that we ended up taking the tour. There's hardly any way to compare what you would learn by just stumbling around vs. being taken under the wing of someone who actually lives here and can really show you more about what it's like.

247

Just remember my oft-repeated advice about the grain of salt: *any* tour guide can only share with you *their* view of things, so listen, learn, and stay open. George, for example, has strong opinions and isn't the least bit shy about speaking his mind. To his credit, he's completely upfront and accepting of this trait, so you're readily forewarned and I don't think he takes it personally if you choose to accept some and discard other parts of his advice. He's definitely going to "tell it like it is" from *his* experiences and point of view.

I'd willing to bet money that *all* of the other tour operators, as well, have some pretty strong opinions and may or may not be as open in acknowledging their prejudices. So it's *your* responsibility to keep your common sense about you and test all things you hear with whether they feel true for you.

One big improvement in George's tour since *we* took it—really the only improvement we felt that it needed—is that it *now* provides the single thing we thought was missing: opportunities to meet and talk with people who have recently moved here—generally people who have taken his tour in the past.

We started hosting dinner for his guests and other gringos who now live in San Ramon, on the first night on their tour, and did that for a couple of years. (At the moment we're taking a break and they're being hosted by our friends, Tom and Susan at Vista

248

ValVerde.) We enjoyed the chance to meet new folks and we all were glad to "pay it forward" by being able to share some of what we'd learned with others as they contemplated making the big move.

I think that Andrew's *Boomers* tour provides some similar opportunities, and I would encourage you to make sure it does if you're going that route—I think it's invaluable. As always, keep an open mind and realize that people's opinions will be varied, and might or might not really match up with what's important to *you*, but in any case the chance for first-hand, current insights will be great, especially since the overwhelming majority of these folks you meet in these social gatherings have nothing to sell you, so they're glad to tell you the "real truth" (at least as far as *they* see it!) and that's a great thing.

Actually, what a good time to mention yet again this issue of the "truth as far as they see it." There's a corollary problem you should be aware of when you talk to folks who live here, especially gringos who have bought a house or, even worse, bought land and built a house. They're understandably "committed" and this *can* color their public statements about the merits—or drawbacks—of where they live. You'd think that if they're not actually selling something, they'd have no motivation to speak anything other than the truth.

But—and it can be a pretty big "but"—some folks just can't bring themselves to say out loud that it *sucks* where they live. It's too cold, it's too windy, it's too cloudy; they constantly battle mold and mildew. These are the realities of living too *high* (in my experience, once you get anywhere close to 4,000 feet, much less 5,000 feet) but if *you* are stuck there, you might not be open about these issues. After all, it's as though that somehow reflects on your own judgment for building your house there.

Or maybe the reality of a place is that it's too hot, too sticky, too humid, too much of a tourist town, too much of a gringo rip-off. *These* are the possible very real complaints of a beach town. But, again, some folks are reluctant to give you this particular version of reality.

And, of course, some people who live up high in the cloud forest genuinely love it, as do some folks at the beach. And the tough part is *how do you tell?* Are they really telling the truth when they say they love it, or are they just making lemonade out of lemons?

Well, I'm sorry to say, there is no great way to tell. Darn, huh? I know you were hoping I was going to share the magic key, but I don't think there is one. I think the best I can offer is something that you'll hear repeated throughout my books (I *know* I've said it several times already in this one!)—take everything you hear with a grain of salt. Does it sound like I'm harping on this point? Perhaps so, but honestly I think this might be the single best piece of advice and insight I can drill into you.

Keep a little open skepticism. Maintain an open mind and really keep your ears open. If one person you talk with in a certain area raves about it, but everyone else you meet in that town talks about the terrible wind in that area, don't let yourself get swept away by their view and *apparent* delight in their area. Do a bit of further legwork. Go visit an area at different times of the day. Try to talk with others, especially those who have experienced other "seasons" there. Keep the "rent before you buy" advice in mind.

I think very few people actually deliberately set out to mislead others. But there are two issues to be aware of. One is simply that one person's wants and needs may just not be in alignment with yours. So they're telling you *their* truth, but it's not going to match yours. The other is the phenomenon I've been speaking of, where they *mean* to be telling you the truth, but they've gone so deeply into their self-protective fantasy that they no longer know what the truth is.

So just be aware. Be a smart consumer. Ask questions. *Listen* to the answers—the spoken parts as well as the unspoken ones. And then use your own head! Remember that the information you find in your research is only *data* for you to use as you make up your own mind. Don't let it *replace* using your own common sense.

—How to Choose a Place to Live

Certainly George Lundquist's tour is designed to both give you an overall view of Costa Rica and what it might be like to live here and also very specifically show you some sample communities in which you might want to settle. As described in more depth in my section on the tour, for us that sampling was enough for us to find our perfect place, and for us it really is "perfect"—using the term advisedly since, of course, perfect is also a function of your attitude and perceptions, not simply geography.

There clearly are, though, physical factors that come into play, and it's been suggested to me that it would be useful to say a bit more about what some of those are.

From all our initial reading, and knowing that we were coming with "medical issues," we had initially felt that we would need to be *very near* San Jose to get the necessary medical care. We learned that while it's true that the major private hospitals are all in the general San Jose area, you certainly don't need to "live" there to have access to that care. Part of what attracted us to

San Ramon was the fact that it does, in fact, have a full-service hospital and a wide array of doctors. We've never once felt "in danger" medically by not being "closer" to the hospitals in San Jose (which are also only an hour away).

Since my parents were college professors and we'd lived the past twenty years near Brunswick, Maine, home to Bowdoin College, we were drawn to "college towns" and that had even initially led us to consider Heredia. As I've mentioned before, we now consider Heredia to be a place we avoid at all costs, so I'm glad we outgrew that notion. But I'll also acknowledge that there are probably folks who live in the smaller communities outside Heredia who are perfectly happy. Me, I'd hate to have to battle the dense traffic, narrow streets, and just general *confusion* of Heredia on my several-times-a-week trips to town, but as with all things, to each their own.

It was that *idea* of a college town, however, that was one of the many factors that turned us on to San Ramon. It houses the "western campus" of the University of Costa Rica. Now that we've been here a while, I have to say that the qualities I usually associate with college towns aren't particularly visible here—the extensive array of international restaurants, the cultural events, the *energy* of several thousand "intellectuals" wandering around town—but having said that, I certainly wouldn't say it's a disadvantage. And we love San Ramon so much that any "failures" it has as a college town are simply non-issues.

We'd also zeroed in on 3,000 feet as our "perfect" elevation, although I have to say I think that was partly just good juju. On the tour, George emphasizes elevation a lot, but he also tends to lump 3,000 to 5,000 feet together as though that were one zone. It is *so* not one zone. Huge differences between 3,000 and 5,000. Again to each their own. Part of *your* task is to figure out what *your* magic zone is.

Because we stumbled onto the town of San Ramon and then onto our wonderful land so serendipitously (and easily, if you don't count David's pain from his banged-up knee!) I tend not to put as much conscious thought into the process as some do. But, a while back, I began corresponding with a woman who had been a participant in George's tour. As a result, I had spoken to her and her husband (and the whole group) on the Monday morning of their tour about shipping. Generally at that presentation I offer some excerpts from these books that will be particularly useful at a practical level, and Michele and I struck up an email conversation coming out of that.

As we started our conversation I asked her for a bit of insight into what they were looking for as far as land went. (She had already told me that they'd nearly bought one piece of land down in San Isidro but had realized—luckily in time!—that there were many problems with the property and the location, so they were now *looking* again.)

She described a lot of features that were somewhat "out of kilter" (in my view) with their budget, so here's what I emailed to her:

> Yeah, I wish we could get pix of the monkeys –
> they're slippery little devils and so far have defied
> photographing! ;-) But we sure do enjoy them.
> And the birds are amazing too. We were never
> "birders" in the states, but I don't see how you
> could *not* be here – we have our own pair of
> toucans, a pair of laughing falcons, endless parrots,
> the wonderful oro pendolas with their brilliant
> yellow tails, and lots and lots of random other birds
> we're only just learning about. It's truly one of the
> special things here, I think!
>
> We're actually at about 3,000 feet which – FOR US!
> – is just perfect. Too much higher and the "cooler"
> weather is measurably cooler, and with more
> clouds and wind, and any lower and the "warmer"
> days are too warm. Atenas, for instance, with its
> supposedly best climate in the world (which
> National Geographic denies having ever said!) is too
> warm for us. But that's the beauty of Costa Rica –

256

it's easy to "tweak" the climate almost exactly to your liking, or at least the "temperature" if not the actual climate! ;-)

River, monkeys, acreage, right climate – frankly you'll be VERY lucky if you find that for $75k. Not to say it couldn't happen, but I'd say that by and large those days are gone here. One piece of [unsolicited!] advice I can offer is to do some thorough discussing and deciding about which factors are your "necessaries" and which are your "would-be-nices". If your budget can go higher, for instance, then you'll have more options. If not (and believe me, I understand "not"), then I don't want to say you have to automatically "give up" on the whole package, but it's REALLY useful to spend some time with yourself (and each other) deciding which are the characteristics that are most important, which ones would you be more willing to give up on. Not to be discouraging, but to help you zero in on the things that will really make you the MOST happy with the place you find.

To this day she still claims this is one of the best pieces of advice she ever received. She and her husband immediately set out to create such a list. (Bear in mind, the final list in some ways is less important than the *process* of thinking about it all, and *talking* about it together if you're coming as a couple. It's all too easy to assume that your mate has the same priorities as you do, and even long married couples can be surprised to find how *un-true* this can be!)

She sent me a list, and within a day had sent a revised list. Clearly the process had invoked discussion. Now, as it turned out, her wish list ended up matching *our* property almost point for point, and we had an interesting situation in which one of the partners in our land had not yet been successful selling his spec houses in Oregon and was starting to feel the pressure of the impending need to close on the land here when he didn't yet have the money in hand from sales up there.

As an evolution from the story told here in this book of our finding and buying the land here, the property had turned into a larger piece of land carrying a larger price. This evolution actually produced a much better property, at a reasonable price for what it was, but it was now out of our budget (using the term "budget" somewhat loosely since, as you'll recall, we too hadn't sold the property we'd expected to). Our solution was to take in partners so that several of us co-own the land (in a corporation) with the shareholders each having "rights" to a designated building site.

It's a slightly "out of the box" situation and it wouldn't have been the right "fit" for most people. But, having seen their wish list which otherwise seemed nearly impossible to fulfill, we broached the subject (tentatively, admitting readily that it was a somewhat strange concept) and everything clicked. We ended up releasing my cousin (our partner) from his commitment and Michele and Paul become our new partners. So in her case, making the list really was a dramatic factor in their buying the land of their dreams.

Your list might be completely different from theirs (which is included at the end of this chapter), and you might still find that your "perfect" property ends up looking very little like your list. A great example is how David and I felt quite strongly that we were looking for some "acreage" and yet initially agreed to buy property with only 1-1/4 acres of land. As I described earlier, it felt so "right" in other ways that we decided to rearrange our priorities. But at least we did so *consciously* and with discussion. How can you be conscious and have discussion, if you don't even have a starting point for what you want?

It's also important to recognize the difference between "easily changed/fixed/added/removed" types of criteria vs. those that are comparatively permanent. The weather, for instance, pretty much is what it is, and buying a property at too high (or too low) an elevation for your desired weather is something you will *never* be able to truly fix. On the other hand, having "hot water" on your required list—found on many people's house

259

criteria, for example—is [a] something you can conceivably get used to doing without and [b] not very expensive or difficult to install in the form of instant hot water heaters.

To paraphrase the Serenity Prayer, recognize the difference between things you can change, and those you can't, and make good decisions accordingly!

What are some factors you might consider when you make *your* list?

I would have to suggest that climate/temperature should be a huge one since that's just not something you can change. Sure, you can mitigate the heat at lower elevations with air conditioning or glass in your porch at higher elevations to block the howling wind, but from watching many people move to Costa Rica (and a fair number leave) I can assure you that determining what kind of weather *you* want will be a most excellent starting point.

Another might be the broader sense of "physical location"—is it important to you to be close to shopping, the private hospitals, certain friends, the beach, the airport, and so forth? While many of those criteria might be satisfied in a number of places, a lot of other places will clearly fail the test, so, again, how do you know which factors will be most important to you if you don't think it out ahead of time.

Like a farm community? Want a town large enough to have a movie theater? Want to be able to eat out at a wide variety of restaurants and buy exotic foods easily?

Do you intend to have a car? It's certainly possible to live here without, but that will (or, at least, *should)* factor into you decision about where to live. Is it on the bus line? Easy for a taxi driver to find? Relatively close to the things you will regularly need or want to do?

Still another type of factor is more about "community" than it is physical characteristics. And this is probably one of the hardest to determine until you're actually here. Do you want to be in a gated community with mostly other ex-pats around? Do you want to be in a Tico community and, if you think you do, you might be sure you're not "idealizing" that—do you speak the language or at least genuinely are doing the work required to learn?

Other friends were seriously investigating moving to Costa Rica and they'd found what they thought was their ideal location (far south, near the Panama border in a small Tico community) when it finally sank in at a true "gut level" that she would probably never be fluent enough in Spanish to do what she really wanted to do. Her passion is health—natural foods, herbs, cleansing, and so forth—and the way she helps people is through genuine, heart-to-heart conversations about their lives.

There's a *huge* difference between being able to chit-chat about the weather and buy things at the market in Spanish vs. having the depth and ease of language necessary for that type of conversation. To their credit, rather than blindly ignoring this fact, they revalued and reorganized their plans, and actually decided that the move *wasn't* the right fit for them after all. They're re-creating their lives in the high desert of New Mexico and are grateful that they didn't go to the expense and headache of moving down and back again.

Do you really feel sure you don't want other gringos around? Remember that "isolation" issue I discussed earlier. How "far away" from other gringos is too far? (Or too close, for that matter!)

This is probably where the oft repeated advice to rent before you buy comes in. It is oft repeated because it's really good advice! The weather you can actually find out about pretty accurately if you'll ask the right questions and truly listen to the answers. (Human nature makes us often be very good about *not* listening, especially if the answer is contrary to what we were hoping for.) Watch for the unspoken answer along with the spoken.

If someone is telling you the temperature is great where they are, but there's a well-used fireplace in sight and you're more "warm-weather" folks, then which answer are you going to listen to? Someone tells you the climate is mild and delightful, but all the houses you see around have glassed in porches, this almost assuredly promises sharp winds, often bringing cool moist air with them. If someone tells you the weather is perfect in their beach town, but you wilt every time you leave their air conditioned home, it's worth remembering that people have differing tolerances for heat (and cold) and the only one that matters is *you.*

But aside from the weather, this sense of the *community* is harder to tell about until you've lived some where for a while. Communities have personalities, and one of the best ways to discover it is to live there and see how it feels. Do you make friends? Are the other ex-pats a welcoming and tolerant group or do you sense a lot of divisiveness and cliques? Do you love the feel of the farmers market and the central park? Do the Ticos reach out to help you or do you get the sense that they've seen a few too many gringos recently? Do the crowded streets seem lively and exciting or dangerous and hostile? There are all kinds of communities here. Find yours!

SMALL FINCA WISH LIST

Essence: Pleasant temperatures with daily sunshine. Abundant wildlife (birds, frogs, pizote, butterflies).

Basics:
- An elevation between 3,000 and 3,600 feet (3,800 max)
- 6,000 sq meters (1.5 acres) or more
- Electricity and water available on/at the edge of the property
- Phone line or cell phone coverage available
- A town with a hospital within a half-hour drive
- One year financing (1/2 at closing, 1/2 a year later) or two-year financing (1/3 at closing, 1/3 in a year, 1/3 in two years) depending on selling price

With at least two of the following:
- Bordering a public road
- Bordering a river (with a flat building site > 15 meters from the river)
- Bordering a reserve
- Primary forest
- Territorial mountain views (with minimal grazing land)

Bonuses:
- Monkeys (howlers or capuchins)
- Internet access
- No visible neighbors
- A small waterfall
- A Nicoya Peninsula view

Frosting:
- An orphanage within a half-hour drive (for volunteering)
- A wildlife rehab center within a half-hour drive (for volunteering)

Deal-breakers ☹
- Lots of mosquitoes or chiggers or no-see-ums
- Few or no trees on the property or neighboring land
- 4x4 required (all-wheel drive okay)
- A pig farm nearby
- Further than 1 ½ hours from the airport

Reprinted with permission

—Budgets

I described in Part One about our efforts to determine if we could afford to make this move and the challenges in obtaining accurate cost information. This is a huge subject that deserves more coverage, and as a result has its own book in the series *(You're Spending How Much?)* due out next year, which will cover a wide variety of folks living different lifestyles.

But for starters, here I'm going to reprint the budget we created in 2006 based on what we'd been able to find out, our *current* typical monthly expenses with a few notes and explanations, and a recent "budget projection" done by our land partners, Paul and Michele, which was the product of lots of input we'd given them from our own expenditures and those of our very good friends, Chris and Louise.

You still read all over the place—from supposedly authoritative sources—how inexpensive it is to live here. I just read something put out by *International Living* magazine that cited sample food costs in Costa Rica and it was laughable. Well, laughable if it weren't sad that people are reading that and believing it to be true. (I can absolutely promise you that you should *not* expect to come here and buy chicken for $0.95 a pound or fish for $1.10 a pound. Maybe three to five times that.)   Although, oddly enough, their utility estimates weren't too far off.   It's like someone went to the grocery store with the wrong currency conversion chart or something.

As "back-up" for the idea that it's cheap to live in Costa Rica, it is universally pointed out that the average Tico makes somewhere between $500 and $700 a month (the exact figure changes but it's always low compared to what almost anyone in North America would consider viable) so it's very easy to get the impression that it *actually* is inexpensive to live here. And there surely are, indeed, gringos living here on $700 or $800 a month, and probably living better than they would in the U.S. *on that amount.*

But, and it's really a *huge* "but" that bears some real listening to, *most* North Americans do not want to live like that.   That is *not* what they're looking for when they come.   Why can Ticos live *happily* on that amount of money and gringos can't?   Let's face it—we're spoiled!

Making the kind of sweeping generalization that always gets one into trouble, we come from a first-world nation where the world is pretty damn advanced.   Most of us would take having hot water throughout our houses absolutely for granted. Most would take having a kitchen filled with modern, functioning appliances for granted, along with a wide assortment of cooking gear and dishware, plus a fridge and pantry full of food. We have a computer (if not several), and high-speed internet.

We have TV sets in practically every room, and if we don't have a TV, it's a matter of "choice" and we're likely to have a home library full of books or a studio full of our crafts or art instead. We routinely buy wine and imported products of all sorts, cheeses and meats for all our meals—unless we're vegetarian in which case the odds are good we spend a lot of money on fancy meat-replacement products. We rarely drive cars that are more than ten years old (and many folks in North America haven't *seen* a ten year old car since, perhaps, their first car in high school or college) and in most households *each* adult has their own car, sometimes more than one.

And all that I've just described applies to most "middle-class" North Americans, not just the wealthiest. We're not even *going there!*

This "average Tico family" that you always read about who lives on a few hundred dollars a month has essentially none of the above. None of it. They might own their own home—in fact, often do—because they built it by hand some years ago on land that was owned

269

by their family. It has tiny rooms and not very many of them, no hot water anywhere (possibly an electric "suicide shower"), very likely not a "real" kitchen stove (with oven) but a counter-top burner, very possibly with a wood stove as well. There is a tin roof with no insulation and vastly sub-standard plumbing and wiring—although this isn't too much of an issue because they don't run dishwashers, Jacuzzi tubs, fancy electronics, or even much in the way of lights other than one bare overhead bulb.

They don't eat "meat" at most meals, and if they do it's likely to be a small bit of inexpensive beef or chicken that's mixed with other ingredients, not a slab of pricey protein that takes up a third of the plate. Most eat rice and beans in some form at two if not all three meals a day. Many consider buying packaged items like toothpaste or breakfast cereal to be a luxury that's indulged in occasionally.

Their electric bill is about $10 to $15 a month, because they don't own the electric hogs—hot water heaters and clothes dryers. They are unlikely to own a car, and if they do it will be one car for the entire family, and it's probably old and very small.

You get the picture. And it's changing. Satellite TV and the internet have brought the outside world in, and the Costa Rica of the past is quickly disappearing. It's also important to realize that there are quite a lot of

Costa Ricans who are living very "gringo" lives. You can go into TGI Friday at noon any day and find it *filled* with Ticos spending $20 or $30 apiece for lunch. There are lots of fancy cars on the road here and they're not all driven by gringos, not by a long shot.

But, and we're back to that word again, they're not the Ticos living on $600 a month that you hear about.

There was a large controversy in the online "forum" community recently when there was a blog posting telling about some gringos who were "living here" on $850 a month. It was being presented, in a sense, as "proof" that it could be done. There was an interesting response from folks crying "foul"—that these people might be doing it (i.e. I don't think anyone claimed they weren't telling the truth) but it wasn't representative of what most people consider "normal" life. They also were, in effect, traveling, not truly settling in to live here long term.

I think the brouhaha was a bit misplaced because the video interview with the couple in question heavily emphasized their decision to become "minimalists" and if repeating the word a dozen times in the video wasn't clear enough, their description of the four light-bulbs that made up almost the entire electrical usage in their home should have been the clue.

So, more power to them (so to speak). It reminded me of times in my past when I've lived aboard sailboats. Similar to these folks, your "worldly possessions" are typically reduced to what will fit in one duffle bag, and it's likely to be a "lifestyle" that people follow for a limited period of time—months, maybe a few years, not forever.

If this is the sort of life adventure that appeals to you, I have zero interest in discouraging you. There are some wonderful things about choosing to live a simple life where you can pack up your duffle bag and move to another part of the world whenever you choose (as the folks in this particular video were doing). This is *not* however, what the majority of people are looking for when they are thinking about moving to Costa Rica. They're more likely thinking of living a lifestyle that will be "recognizable" to them as perhaps not *exactly* the same, but *similar* to how they've always lived.

This is human nature. And, personally, I don't think it needs to be apologized for. But it should be recognized so that you're being realistic about whether this is a move that's a good fit for you. And, for most people, one essential starting point is financial—can you afford to live the life you want here in Costa Rica? Or, perhaps, put another way, what kind of life can you afford to live, here or elsewhere?

Hopefully these budgets will give a good starting point. The following three pages show our projected budget we made in 2006 before we moved, our actual expenses from January 2010, and a recently prepared, very thorough projection for a more typical couple.

Note that the spreadsheet showing our January expenses is a somewhat randomly selected month where we managed to keep track of every penny we spent. Most expenses are pretty consistently recurring so it gives a good sense of our actual monthly expenses. Note this particular month had no major car repairs, no "traveling expenses" or other major purchases.

Income and Expense Projections — 2006, prior to actually moving to Costa Rica

Initial Income

Wu-SS	1,400.70
Phyl-SS	506.70
AmEx Annuity	480.68
TIAA-CREF	1,528.19
	3,916.27
DCB SS	1,075.00
Household Total	$ 4,991.27

	Anticipated Actual Cost	Conservative Monthly Allowance			Excess Income
			Total Anticipated	2,942.55	2,048.72
Initial Expenses - Phase One			Total Allowance	4,158.05	833.22
Rent	350.00	500.00			
Groceries 25 pp/wk (40 pp/wk)	430.00	688.00			
Doctor's Visits	80.00	140.00			
Medicine	100.00	140.00	Will be free w/in 3 to 6 mo. with residency		
Hired Help	350.00	500.00			
Auto Expenses	90.00	120.00			
Misc. Expense	150.00	250.00			
Electricity	25.00	50.00			
Water	4.50	7.00			
Phone	35.00	60.00	(2 cells + Skype or similar)		
Internet	40.00	150.00			
TV (Satellite)	35.00	100.00			
Air Amb. Trav. Ins.-Wu	60.42	60.42			
Air Amb. Trav. Ins.-Phyl	60.42	60.42			
Air Amb. Trav. Ins-D&A	65.42	65.42			
Potential payment on LOC	300.00	500.00			
LTC Insurance -Wu	203.41	203.41			
LTC Insurance -Phyl	147.84	147.84			
Medicare Supp. Ins.	138.00	138.00			
Medicare Supp. Ins.	277.55	277.55			

ASSETS/CASH FLOW

Cash/money mkt/mutual fund	53,000
IRA- Wu	21,000
IRA-Phyl	17,000
Cash draw capacity of HELOC**	50,000 ** Home Equity Line Of Credit

	ASKING	MORE CONSERVATIVE
House	337,000	285,000
Lot 1	50,000	40,000
Lot 2	50,000	40,000
Lot 4	70,000	60,000
	507,000	425,000

LIABILITIES/EXPENSES

Mortgage	160,000	160,000
Misc short term debt of W&P	8,000	8,000
Home Equity payback if drawn	50,000	50,000
Subdivision Costs*	15,000	18,000
Moving costs	15,000	20,000
Real estate commission	20,220	17,100

* $10,000 in surveyor/engineer fees + $5,000 fire pond

Brink actual expenses, January 2010

Groceries	1,016	includes 3 people all meals, 5 people many meals
Electricity	227	daily use of clothes dryer; hot water heater
Phone	23	
Vonage (U.S. phone)	35	two cell phones
DISH TV	90	
Gasoline	100	
Propane	12	
Payroll	871	housekeeper and caregiver for mom; coffee picking
CAJA--medical	218	David/Arden; mom; housekeeper
Doctor/Pharmacy	673	
Macrobiotica	23	supplements
Eating out	69	
Marchamo (due in Dec)	112	paid in December from January money
Maine tax pmt	50	
Chase credit card pmt	150	
Misc purchases	404	misc smalls plus $200 for pantry shelves
eFax service	17	
Trash	15	
Aerocasillas	52	monthly fee plus charges for items received
ATM fees	30	
Bank fees	58	
AARP	178	additional insurance, mom; need to cancel
loan pmt to PM	100	paying off a former business debt
$	4,523	

Projected Annual Living Expenses, 2010

DESCRIPTION	MONTHLY	ANNUALLY	TOTAL
FOOD	400.00		4,800.00
ALCOHOL	150.00		1,800.00
UTILITIES			
Electricity	150.00		1,800.00
Propane	15.00		180.00
Water	8.00		96.00
Garbage	15.00		180.00
Bank fees	50.00		600.00
Internet	60.00		720.00
Mail	15.00		180.00
Cell phone	10.00		120.00
VEHICLE			
Gas	150.00		
Marchamo		1,000.00	1,000.00
Repairs		1,000.00	1,000.00
Liability Insurance		150.00	150.00
MEDICAL			
CAJA insurance	80.00		960.00
Prescriptions	150.00		1,800.00
Doctor, dentist, etc.		1,000.00	1,000.00
HOUSEKEEPER 10hrs/wk	120.00		1,440.00
GARDENER 15hrs/wk	180.00		2,160.00
TRAVEL			
Airfare to the States		3,000.00	3,000.00
Mini-vacations in CR		2,000.00	2,000.00
MISCELLANEOUS	150.00		1,800.00
TOTAL ANNUAL			26,786.00
TOTAL MONTHLY	2,250.00		
ADDITIONAL 1st YEAR			
Rent	600		7200.00
Storage	300		3600.00
			10800.00

Reprinted with permission, Paul and Michele G.

—Reality Check

Is there any real way to know for sure if this is a good move for you? The truthful answer is "no." (Sorry, I know that's not the answer you were looking for!)

Sometimes even folks who seemed quite sure it would be a good fit find that it's not. But, just as I've hinted at throughout this book, there *are* some signals, some personal sign-posts that are likely to offer you some good guidance if you actually pay attention to them.

So, let's see if I can help you step back for a bit of reality check.

First might simply be to look at *why* you're thinking of moving to Costa Rica in the first place. For some, this might be enough to clarify that it's a bad idea. You're desperately unhappy where you are? Not likely to find that a move to a foreign country changes that. You know the old saying, "wherever you go, there you are." This is particularly true when you move far away from home. A geographic change is rarely the answer for deep depression, anxiety, or despair.

We had a poignant experience of this right here in our little local community when we had a friend who had opened his home to someone he'd met who was very interested in moving to Costa Rica. She had been here for a few weeks and had met up with a number of the other local gringos at various events. She had seemed fairly "average" and "normal" in casual interactions, although later some folks did comment that her eyes seemed somewhat oddly *vacant*. But certainly nothing that alarmed anyone. She spoke of her plans to return to Florida in a few days and a job she was hoping to get.

Perhaps you can imagine our collective shock to find that just a couple of days after she'd been in our home at a party, she choose a time in the afternoon when our friend would be out running errands, left some money for things that would need to be done, and went into his back yard and shot herself.

To say we were stunned is an understatement. I still feel a little ripple of shock even writing this, now more than a year later. To our knowledge, this was not a case of experiencing one specific devastating thing while she was here that pushed her over the edge, but clearly she was someone who had a deep unhappiness and despair that she hid pretty well.

While the event sparked some local controversy over everything from owning a gun to meeting people over the internet to the concept of responsible journalism (there was some pretty *irresponsible* stuff published at the time), it unequivocally demonstrated a hugely important fact—if you're desperately unhappy and depressed where you currently live, coming to Costa Rica will *not* fix that. Depression and suicidal thoughts are a serious matter. Get the help you need and don't think hopping on a plane will solve your problems.

Of course, on the other hand, if you simply feel a bit stuck and stagnant where you are, you might well find that the challenges and excitement of a move like this is just what you need to get the blood going again. So be honest with yourself about where you are now and why you want to move.

Another *huge* issue to face up to honestly is your financial situation.

Do you have enough resources and income to manage the actual *cost* of the move and cover your ongoing living expenses? Certainly people move to Costa Rica on a tight budget, perhaps even tight enough that 10-grand to ship their stuff is out of reach financially. I completely understand this and recognize that doesn't automatically mean you can't do it.

But please do be realistic about what you are going to do when you get here and you need to then *buy* all that stuff. Maybe you can truly get by just fine and you'll find a fully furnished apartment or house. You tuck a few personal treasures into your suitcase (remembering that the days of shipping many excess pieces of luggage are generally gone) and you're good to go.

But many folks simply don't think it all the way through. They imagine buying the absolute basics here and say "oh that'll be fine, that's all I need" and maybe that's true for the first few months. But if you're really going to live here for years to come, perhaps even the rest of your life, is that really how you want to live? There's no right or wrong answer to that question, except for the answer that is *right* for *you*.

Financially, too, it's important to make the distinction between resources (or assets) and income. Most people will need to tap into their assets in some way to financially manage the move. Typically, they'll sell a house or some other investment and some of those proceeds will finance the shipping and the other costs of "settling in" here.

But then there's the issue of monthly expenses and so much has been written about how *inexpensive* it is to live here that people often come down with unrealistic expectations about how lavishly they'll live on their $1,500 a month income.

As I've said elsewhere in this book, yes, I think it probably *is* true that you can make any given amount of income stretch further here in Costa Rica than almost anywhere in the U.S. or Canada. The weather alone can have a huge economic impact in a country where there are plenty of places to live that require neither heating nor air conditioning. (Don't expect to live at the beach and be comfortable without air conditioning unless you have some serious experience with hot, humid environments and you know for a fact that you're happy being sweaty and sticky all the time.)

During our last year before we left Maine, our *year-round* payment plan for our fuel oil was $500 a month. That was over five years ago and would have been much higher some of these past years that we've lived here, if we'd stayed there instead. That $6,000 to $10,000 a year in fuel oil alone is enough of a savings to make a difference in most people's budgets!

But, at the same time, we've not found it to be quite as "cheap" to live here as we'd imagined, especially in a few key areas. Food, for instance. We spend nearly the same amount here as we did 4+ years ago in the states. Now, maybe food has really gone up in price in the states and we're spending much less than we *currently* would have been spending in the states. It's hard to judge that. But I can sure say it's nowhere near the *fraction* of our U.S. budget that we'd been imagining.

Again, reality check time: do you truly want to

live and eat like a Tico, or is the "thrill" of that lifestyle change going to wear off after a while and you'll return to a somewhat more familiar way of cooking and eating?

I have met almost no Tico who doesn't eat rice and beans every day, for at least one meal a day, sometimes all three (perhaps in slightly varied form). Conversely, I have not met one gringo who is even willing to eat rice and beans every day, much less at all three meals. For most of us, after all, it's *not* how we've spent the previous many decades of our lives eating. It's not to say one way is better than the other, but it is foolish to pretend to yourself that you are suddenly going to eat like a Tico—for the *rest of your life!*—when it's exceedingly unlikely that that will be the case.

I'm actually not trying to harp on food, per se, here. Just maybe you really are the only gringo around who is going to be delighted eating nothing but rice and beans forever. The point is, *be realistic* about how you really want to live and plan your finances accordingly. If you have a very limited budget, you will likely find you can make it stretch further here than in the U.S. or Canada but it's almost assuredly going to mean some serious lifestyle adjustments.

Another financial area where you sure want to have a bit of "reality check" is around medical expenses and how you will cover them. You read everywhere about the CAJA and the "free" medical services and prescription drugs, but what you often don't read is about how overburdened that system is and how few "modern" drugs are covered by the CAJA. So while the system is great for emergencies, it does *not* eliminate (for most gringos) the need for private-pay medical care.

If you have a heart attack or go into anaphylactic shock after an ant bite (as a friend of ours recently did), you will probably find that the CAJA provides excellent quality medical care. The facility is likely to look like a 1950s hospital, but the equipment is more than adequate and the skill of the doctors and nurses is topnotch.

However—and for most folks it's a huge "however"— you're likely to find that if you need medical procedures that are *not* "life and death" they'll be scheduled months into the future. You might be fine with waiting nine months for that angioplasty, but lots of people aren't.

And all those "designer drugs" to control your high blood pressure, your enlarged prostate, your cholesterol, and so on are *not* likely to be covered by the CAJA. Now, personally, I think you should consider some alternatives to some of that anyway, and I *don't* simply mean different drugs, but hey, that's just me. And when you need medications you need them, right, so now you're going to be paying for them at any of the zillions of private *farmacias* (pharmacies) that are to be found sprinkled generously through most any town.

Our budget has to include over $400 a month for the medications that David needs for his blood pressure, heart, and prostate—all pretty common for a 68 year old man—plus thyroid medicine for our golden retriever, Hannah. And that's just the monthly routine expenditures. Sprinkle a few random illnesses in there, a urinary tract infection or two, and a sciatica flare-up, and average that over the year, and we spend easily $500 to $600 a month on "medical" of some sort.

If you have a chronic health condition, are the medications you need going to be available to you here? It's not just the cost that needs to be considered, but also the availability. While most things *are* available, *all* are not and it's best not to assume. On one of your exploratory trips to Costa Rica, go to a pharmacy with your list and see if you can get what you need (and what it will cost), then factor that into your planning.

Most medical procedures here are vastly less expensive than in the states, but if you're going to have to pay for them out-of-pocket—which you likely will— then you need to be sure those pockets hold sufficient resources to be able to do so.

If you're old enough for Medicare, one "back-up" plan is to presume that in a pinch you could return to the U.S. and have medical procedures done there.

Medicare (at least at this time) does *not* provide any coverage out of the country, but if you have medical needs that aren't of an "emergency" nature and you'd be well enough to travel, going home to visit the kids and grandkids and planning that cataract surgery or hip replacement is not a bad plan.

What about a seven-week course of radiation for that throat cancer? How are you going to pay for that when the time comes? Hopefully, of course, that time *won't* come, but it's sure important to think out how you would cope if it did.

Mom and Dad had some modest investments that gave them the back-up they needed, and in fact covered Daddy's brain surgery, his later (and final) several week hospitalization for pneumonia and kidney failure, and an out-patient surgery for Mom to remove a cyst. Those medical expenses pretty much wiped out their investments, but in some ways that wasn't any problem—after all, that's what the funds were for: to cover an emergency!

On the other hand, *we* don't have much of anything in the way of savings, so will be having to rely on the CAJA or a return to the U.S. We've thought that through and decided we can live with that, and maybe you can too. But you need to go through the mental exercise and be sure!

We've been talking a lot about finances. What if

you don't actually *have* an ongoing monthly income? You want to move to Costa Rica and are planning on *earning a living* here?

I'm sorry to say that I don't have very good news for you. You are almost doomed to failure.

That's pretty harsh, you say? In my world of advising people about shipping, I occasionally get inquiries from folks who want to ship something other than their own personal household goods. A little while ago I'd emailed with someone who was wondering about importing cars to resell. Here's what I had to say to him:

> Okay, it's *technically* possible to bring in vehicles and sell them for a profit, but I will tell you frankly that the several folks we've known who tried this all gave up in despair eventually. There are a couple of immediate problems. One, it's pretty "cash intensive" since you (obviously) have to front the funds to buy the cars, then pay the duty, advertising, carrying costs, etc.
>
> The biggest problem, though, is that while there *is* a market here for good, solid, quality cars from North America, when you go to sell them here you're having to fight against the "traditional" used car here.
>
> The classic Tico used car was purchased by a used-car

dealer as a junker – literally, an insurance write-off with a salvage title in the U.S. – crammed 4 or even 6 to a container (they're already smashed, it doesn't matter) and then "fixed up" here. Even after the repairs, they can be sold for much less than "market value" since they were bought for essentially nothing. THAT's what you're competing against.

So, yes, it can be done. No I don't recommend it. (And it's unfortunate, since I think there is a desperate need for solid used cars here, but the realities of the business are more than most folks are prepared to deal with.)

This particular client replied with appreciation for my frankness, but went on to say he and a buddy were trying to figure out a business to do here. What was my advice, they asked. It's a not-uncommon question, so I'm going to repeat here basically what I told them.

It's hard to think of business opportunities that are "obvious" easy money-makers. I continue to think there are markets here for "specialty" shops that bring in true "gringo" items—both hard goods like furniture and hardware etc. and consumables—specialty food items, "drugstore" type items, "natural living" items, garden items like compost tumblers, and so on.

But there are obvious issues of import permits, business licenses, employees, and the like which can be pretty daunting. So, a lot of upfront capital and difficult to do? Sounds not-so-appealing after all.

In a similar vein, there's potentially a market for importing some very specific building materials—some of the more exotic items like the fully-opening walls of glass (like Lanai doors or Nana glass walls) for instance. But again these are businesses with a substantial start-up investment and the same hassles with licensing, employees, etc.

It seems there's some potential market here in the growing awareness of "real food"—organic/pastured meat (i.e. beef, chicken, pork, bison, etc.), quality cheese, true artisan bread, the kinds of "food" that one might find in a North American "health food store" and so on. Yet again, however, this would be a business fraught with dealing with the various regulatory bodies in a foreign land.

(I assume you're seeing some pattern here.)

The car thing seems "obvious" but, as I shared, we've actually been pretty "close" to a number of these schemes and everyone attempting them has bailed out in various states of financial ruin. So *maybe* it could work, but I'd be hugely skeptical.

Most gringo businesses here are *service* businesses and make a very modest living. Hospitality enterprises—B & Bs, inns, restaurants, tours, and the like—sometimes do well, but there's a world of "issues" with all the hiring and tax implications and, again, lots of people who try these things end up losing their shirts.

What people *can* do well with is an internet based business that they could do from anywhere. There are sure a lot of "get-rich-quick" scams in that realm, however, so you'd want to stay away from those, but if you already have a solid internet business, then that can very likely continue here.

A few folks come and achieve a moderate income flying under the radar offering their psychology services, acupuncture, interior design, health coaching, or whatever. And certainly folks who do consulting or offer professional services where their geography is irrelevant do fine here.

The simple reality is that many (actually, probably, *most)* folks who come down here *needing* to earn a living end up going home. It's just not an easy thing in a place where you can't "get a job."

Not completely impossible, but pretty close to it. If you're coming here and need to earn a living—come with your eyes wide open, some good planning under your belt, and a solid back-up plan.

As a final mental exercise, it's good to revisit Chapter 4 of this book, and then be brutally honest with yourself. Do your friends lovingly describe you as "wound a little tightly"? Does your life revolve around a certain type of social activity or hobby that you won't be able to do here? Are you deeply involved in the day-to-day lives of your grandchildren? Are you truly terrified of spiders? There is nothing wrong with any of these situations, but they might make this a miserable move for you.

Does that mean you have to give up on your dream to move to Costa Rica? Of course not. But why not be among the few smart ones who come down for a trial run of maybe six months or a year. Rent out your house or put your stuff in storage for a while and come on down and rent a furnished place. It won't be *quite* the same as living here "for real"—there's usually still a slight "vacation" quality to that type of experience—but it's the closest you're likely to get to seeing if it works for you.

For some, they knew within the first few months that living in Costa Rica wasn't going to work for them. Quite a lot of others actually stay for several years before deciding to go back. Sometimes it's the cumulative effect of small irritations. The pervasive petty crime got to them. They found they could never really learn Spanish and got tired of not being able to communicate.

Sometimes life just took a radical change—often

when elderly parents needed more assistance than could be managed from afar or a health issue of their own came along that they preferred to handle back in the states. Or they found being single here was just too draining after all without having someone to share the adventure (and frustrations) with.

Lots of possible reasons, and I actually will close this book in the next chapter with some brief stories from a few who have returned.

None of this is meant to be discouraging. I'm a big believer in having and following your dreams. We did, and we love it here. Had we been *too* cautious or paid too much attention to any "negatives" we read, maybe we wouldn't have come, and I would consider that to be tragic!

But I do think that an even greater tragedy is when folks who clearly needed to stop and take a reality check—but didn't bother to do so—blindly forge ahead, liquidating assets when they shouldn't have, quitting jobs they wish they hadn't, wasting significant sums of money to ship down (and then back again), or even worse didn't *have* the money to ship back and found themselves selling off their personal treasures just to finance their return to the states and a potentially bleak financial future. So be smart—take a moment to listen to *both* your head and your heart, especially if they're telling you different things!

If you go through your own "reality check" and find that it still seems like a great idea, then come on down! There's lots of folks here who will be happy to offer a helping hand, people like us who love it here and are glad for the opportunity to "pay it forward" and help others.

If the outcome of your reality check isn't as clear as you might like, then consider some alternate ideas. Come down for a year to check it out, or maybe even just a few months to start. Make a plan that allows for the potential that you'll want to return to your homeland after a few years. Be willing to be flexible. Just as it takes a certain amount of courage to make an international move like this, it also takes a lot of courage to *let go* of the idea if you're finding that it doesn't feel right for you.

Hopefully—with the help of this book—you'll have gotten some real information to help fuel your desire to move to Costa Rica. And if this book has helped put out the fire of that desire and made you realize that a different path was the better one for you, then it's done its job as well. In either case, I wish you well and hope that I've helped. Please feel free to get in touch and let me know!

—A Few Folks Who Moved Back

As I mentioned in Chapter 2, when *I* was researching, the last thing I wanted to hear about was anyone moving *back* to the U.S. It seemed that if someone had moved back, then maybe my plans to move down were ill-advised, and I did *not* want to hear that!

So I'm now going to tell you not to "do as I do" but rather do as I say. We were lucky. We love it here. But I've come to see that an unwillingness to look at the potholes and wrinkles, not just at the joys and adventures, is *not* a smart approach. Obviously you can simply skip over this chapter. I'll never know. But I encourage you to read on. Making a good decision comes with *informing* yourself, not just *selling* yourself!

This is by no means an exhaustive review of different situations that send people back to the U.S. It does give a little glimpse into the thought processes of a few who came... and then went back. Some pretty quickly, some after some years. Read what they have to say....

—Sally O'Boyle

I mention Sally O'Boyle in my earlier chapter about our research before moving here. Her blog (http://www.abroadincostarica.com) was a great source of info to us in our research phase, and I enjoyed reading her stuff over the nearly-five years since then. Sally and her family are an interesting example of several "situations" all rolled into one, so I'd asked her to write something for me to include here. She agreed and then also posted it to her new blog (http://www.fiftytolife.com) where she's generally focusing on re-settling in to the states and her growing involvement in health and the "real food" movement (a topic that's grown in interest for me over the past few years, too!) so you should check out both blogs.

So, here it is, in Sally's own words:

Some eh-Splainin'

When an expat moves back to the native kingdom from their selected soil, gossip hell breaks loose in local forums and coffee shops. Everyone wants to know: "Why?" Since at least 90% of ex-expats never eh-splain why, the rest of us ponder aloud, hoping we are not next in the long line of "expat failures." *¡Qué vergüenza!* Indeed.

Well, I don't feel like a failure. I feel like a huge winner: I got to move from what has always been considered the greatest country on the planet (in many ways, it still is) to the sweetest country on the planet and live a great life for five years. I got to meet and become friends with fantastic people, see places and wildlife and have truly magical adventures I would never have otherwise. I learned to speak Spanish, **almost died**, then lived to tell it all. Failure? Hardly.

But leave we did. Here's why:

1. Money. My illness cost over half our net worth, which wasn't that much before I got sick. We worked all the years we lived in Costa Rica. Despite our best efforts, our income never quite caught up to our outgo and the life was a steady drain on savings. **We only came for a year,** planning to return to **my real estate** income and the old life after a brief adventure. Except, at the end of that first year, my U.S. income had slipped even farther away. There was no money in real estate, save in property management, which I was doing from Costa Rica. Since life was still cheaper in Costa Rica, returning to Key West didn't make sense. Besides, we were happy in CR.

Even so, if we hadn't moved this year, we would have had to in another year if the income picture stayed the same. Money does not grow on trees. I did not want to actually go broke in Costa Rica. Being poor there was one thing; being broke quite another. If I was going to go flat broke, I wanted to be around family and friends. Specifically, around my rich criminal defense attorney brother. Everyone should have one. My getting sick simply hastened our departure.

2. Getting so sick so fast freaked me the hell out. Happy as I was in Costa Rica, as much as I love my Costa Rica friends and the life, my homesickness never fully abated. When I got out of the hospital, all I wanted was to be near my family and life-long friends. I wanted it so badly, I could feel it in every fiber. Like ET, my being felt drawn home. (Yeah, ok, so sometimes I tend toward the dramatic. I have **a degree in it**, after all.)

3. I wanted to work. I'd been antsy for months. I wanted to do something more with my life. I wasn't ready to retire or earn my living staring at a computer screen. I wanted to work outside the house, not necessarily in real estate. I really wanted to do something in the health and wellness field: like acupuncture. Like **ortho-bionomy**. Like pursue this blog idea. Nothing like almost dying to gel your dreams.

4. The boys needed to move on with their lives. I blogged about this one already. It is difficult for **an expat teen to move on in a foreign country**, particularly when they have remnants of a life back in their native land. It pulls. They did not choose Costa Rica. They love Costa Rica, they miss it a lot, they look forward to visiting next spring, but they were

ready to live in the homeland for awhile. Get driver's licenses, GEDs, higher education, jobs that pay decent money, be within driving distance of their lifelong buds and extended family. They are American kids. They need to be here for awhile, then make their own choices.

5. The final straw was that my mom needed me here. She was in the hospital right after I was, twice. She needed care and assistance. My siblings and their spouses all live here, but work full-time jobs. No one could really be there for Mom as much as she needed it. End of analysis: **we moved.**

This was the right move for us. It's been expensive and stressful to move and buy everything new, but that's the price, isn't it? The risk. It was well worth it. Besides, there's an (exciting) new job on the horizon (more on that when I actually have it). The property management team is growing and we have a good system in place, so I still don't have to be there. I am enrolled in acupuncture school starting in January. I'm loving the new blog, plus I can still visit **the old one**! We are all loving being around my family and will visit Key West and all those "old buds" in the spring.

I'm still homesick for Costa Rica and my new friends, but I will see them again. Like Hal likes to say, "How can I miss you if you won't go away?" So, we are gone for a bit, just long enough to miss and be missed, but not for good. Heavens no, we gotta get back and build our **earthbag house** at **Ginnee's farm!**

—Marcia Boyce

Wes and Marcia moved to Puriscal from Las Vegas in March of '09. As far as I knew they were happy here, so I was surprised a little less than eighteen months later when I got an email from her looking for a quote to ship back to the U.S.

In many ways, Wes and Marcia represent a classic case of what can happen when both partners in a relationship are simply not on the same page about living here. When I first asked if she would write something for inclusion in this book, her reply was, "I will be happy to put some thoughts on paper about our likes and dislikes of the Costa Rica experience. Wes loves it, I don't, that sums it up but I will go into detail for you."

Here's that "detail" she promised, in her words. (Bear in mind that all of these stories are direct and honest reports from people, representing the "truth" as they know it. It's entirely possible that not everyone would agree with all statements made, but look for the essence in all the stories and

I think you'll find something helpful in all of them!)

Wes and I were put in a position back in the fall of 2008 to no longer be able to take our monthly retirement payment out of our 401K. We quickly had a HUGE LOSS that made it dangerous to continue taking any money out. It no longer replaced itself and we were worried about depleting it before we died! Soooooo, we started researching CR and decided to give it a try. As you know Las Vegas is and was the worst housing and employment market in the U.S. We were both in favor of giving this a try. I wanted to keep our things in storage in Las Vegas just in case I wanted to go back. Wes said absolutely not, I couldn't keep a foot in each country so here we are, lock, stock, and barrel.

I have always been close and involved in my children's and grandchildren's lives; Wes has not been connected to his kids for years and couldn't care less. I guess it's a man thing. (We have been married 21 years, I had 2 children, 3 grandchildren and now 2 great grandchildren and Wes has 2 children and 6 grandchildren) He has trouble remembering their names, I know all birthdays, schools, etc. So here is one BIG problem.

THE NEGATIVES (MY OPINION)

1. I am disappointed in the medical care (unless we pay for

it.) Primitive facilities, poor substitutes for our prescriptions (even if we pay for it.) The CAJA facility looks like something out of the 1920s.

2.The infrastructure is pathetic, roads, bridges, etc. No addresses, no street names, no street signs, everything seems to be crumbling and falling down. The beaches are not pretty, dogs pooping right in front of your chair, some are polluted, lots of rip tides.

3. Groceries that we Gringos like are twice as much as in the states, our grocery bill is our biggest expense and to get these Gringo things we have to drive for an hour to shop at the Auto Mercado in Escazu.

4. We purchased private health insurance which is not much cheaper than in the states and the first time I tried to use it they refused to honor it. They are now searching the country to see if I have ever had an xray on my baby finger, who knows how many years that will take to get the answer so I can have the painful spurs removed from it. I think the INS is a scam, everything is PRE-EXISTING!

5. We have not been able to communicate very well as our Spanish is not coming along as we expected it would. We were mis-led by statements that English is a required subject

in school and most people can speak English. We have found most offices that we need to do business in don't even have any English speaking employees. YIKES!!! We have to pay a bilingual friend to help us do business.

6. It costs more to buy and build in this country than in the states (and with sub-standard quality and materials quite often).

7. I don't feel there is any qualified trained police protection here. (Wes has never felt that he needed it so I guess it's not important)

8. The constant interruption of water and power is irritating.

9. CR beef is lousy and imported American beef is VERY expensive (although available.)

10. There's not much to do here after you have been to the beach and seen the volcano.

POSITIVES (WES)

1. The views are breathtaking and everywhere

2. It's peaceful and tranquil. The greed factor and keeping

up with the Jones is not here.

3. The weather is perpetual spring at this altitude (3400 ft) no need for heat or air conditioning.

4. Fruit and vegetables are more flavorful and cheap. Rice and beans are plentiful!

5. Interruption from power, water, and phone service is trivial.

6. We're not submerged in all the daily, politically-correct hypocrisy.

7. Ticos are extremely friendly and helpful to not needing to learn Spanish.

8. We can get the house cleaned every week for 5000 colones and a pedicure for 3000 colones.

9. Gardener for yard and trash is just 20,000 colones per month, includes planting and weeding and mowing.

10. We don't have the taxes that we paid in the states.

I hope you will be able to find something of use in this rant from me, bottom line, Wes is happy and quite satisfied with his life here and I am not.

─ Mae Worth

I "met" Mae by email in '06, before we'd even made our move (although we were well on our way!) and we'd stayed in touch. She ended up renting a house on the other side of San Ramon, so we saw each other a few times a year.

I'll let her tell her story in her words, but I think she's a pretty good example of someone who initially liked it here, found it to be an adventure, but in the end, it was just "too much." When I'd initially asked her about going back, she said she was just tired of everything being "so hard." As I've already commented earlier in the book, I think it can, indeed, be much harder to weather the transition to living here when you're on your own. Just having a partner to share the daily challenges (and victories) with can make a lot of difference.

After considering various options, Mae ended up returning to St. Louis, which is where she'd moved here from. I actually had to ask Mae a couple of different times if she would be willing to write something for this book, not because she was "lazy" or anything about answering me, but I think because she found the whole topic to be painful, a form of re-living difficult experiences and it took a little "time and space" for her to be able to do so. I really appreciate her honesty and willingness to open up in the hope that her story may help others.

Mae's story, in her words:

> Living in Costa Rica for three years was the adventure I was looking for, but, it was just one of the adventures in my life.
>
> On Feb 22, 2006, I heard a broadcast on NPR, about Retiring Abroad.
> http://www.onpointradio.org/shows/2006/02/20060222_b_main.asp
>
> This was the beginning of my Costa Rica experience. I researched many books and read information and blogs on the internet for almost a year before my first trip to Costa Rica. At that time, there were few blogs and books written by expats who had made the journey. And some have since made the same decision as I have...to return to the states to live. Now, there are many more blogs, and vlogs (video

blogs), recording their experiences, and challenges. These can all be helpful, but each one's experience is totally unique to their lives, and yours will be also. I found blogging my journey from beginning to end was helpful, not only to others, but as a journal for my memories of Costa Rica, both positive and not so.

Near the end of Nov 2006, my visit to Costa Rica was not a tourist experience. I stayed with a local family, ate meals with them, and very quickly realized that immersion was a great way to learn the language. My college Spanish was of no use to me, could not remember much, and found myself relying on my Italian, which I had learned while living in Italy. The family walked or used taxis to go everywhere. We used the bus system to go into San Jose to again walk around to all the major areas there. The trip was enjoyable, and I felt I could make the adjustments to live there.

In early 2007, I moved lock, stock and yarn stash to Los Angeles, near San Ramon. Living there, I loved the weather, most of the time (rainy season can be pretty brutal), and the beauty of the hills and valleys are breath taking. There is a large expat community in that area, making it easy to have a social life with other Americans. I felt very much a part of this community, as well as a part of the local Tico community.

Living in a foreign country, even with the nice weather and beauty, has its challenges. There were physical challenges, adjustments to diet, less facilities and more difficult to find what I needed. For me, being single meant I had to face each challenge alone. I truly understand the necessity there for living as a family, even for an extended period of time. After a few years, the challenges of living, and missing family, friends, and a more comfortable way of life, I decided to return to the states. Not that my life in the states is without its challenges, they are just more manageable. And yes, having a full understanding of what is being said, or being able to fully communicate makes life less stressful.

The cost of living was not one of my considerations, as for me, I found it almost a wash to live in Costa Rica as living in the metro area of St. Louis. One thing costing more here, may be less there, but the opposite is true also. Only living on the basics, as the Ticos do, would make it less. As Americans, we are blessed, we have much more than most Ticos.

If you wish, you many include my blog site. They may find it helpful also. I will have it updated soon.
http://hopetoliveincr1day.blogspot.com/

—Tom Ackley

Of all the folks who we know who have returned to the states, the news that our friend, Tom Ackley, was to be one of them without a doubt "hit" the hardest. We were actually stunned, as were the friends who had told us about seeing Tom and Susan's place advertised for sale. They had assumed that we knew and asked us about it, but we had nothing to offer except a profound sense of shock.

Why were we so shocked? I think that unlike some of the others where there had been various hints over time, we'd all presumed that Tom and Susan were deliriously happy here. Tom was one of the first gringos we met when we arrived in the fall of '06. We've remained friends through the years since, sharing many holidays and other events together and had always had the impression that they were here for the long haul. (This is actually an interesting example of "human nature" where we tend to assume that other people's "life plans" match our own, even if they'd never actually *said* so.)

We weren't alone in our shock. When we passed the news on to our dear friends, Chris and Louise, we— like the friends who'd initially mentioned it to us—

assumed that *they* must know and have been sworn to secrecy or something. They were closer to Tom and Susan than we were, both geographically (literally living in the same development) and then, we presumed, socially. It turns out that they not only didn't already know, but were at least as stunned as we were, if not more so.

When I queried Tom, he replied right away that it wasn't any "big thing"—even saying that they'd never intended to settle in here forever but, rather, take it on as a "project" for a period of time. The term "five year plan" was bandied about a bit, although I suspect what he wrote below describes it a little more accurately when he said, "We came here with the commitment to stay until we decided to either stay some more, or leave and do something else." The time has come for them to begin to make plans to leave and I'll let him tell the story:

> My wife, Susan, and I bought a fine piece of property in 2004. We had the luxury of packing the container we bought, over several months. I came ahead of Susan, rented a wonderful house with great views only 5 minutes from our property.
>
> Arden has asked that we write a bit about our motivations in moving to Costa Rica, and the accompanying

reasons to leave. I retired young. At the age of about 55, I was ready for a new project. My partner, Susan Lyons, after having worked for 30+ years as a legal administrator, was ready for a change, too. I had always had an interest in Latin culture. Costa Rica has the best infrastructure in Latin America. Over an eighteen-month period, I made five trips here, and looked at literally hundreds of properties. During that time, I spent nearly four months in-country. When I found the piece I ultimately bought, I signed an option to buy it within 15 minutes. That was in October '05. The plan was to build ourselves a home, a large workshop with two bedrooms, and two cabins, for starters, and operate a bed and breakfast. We committed to each other, and the project, five years, as a minimum, with an on-going "review" and evaluation process between us.

The property had no roads, no power, and no water. It was bare, beautiful land, with fabulous views. Though it took over eight months to finally get our building permit, we moved into our little abode (without it having windows or doors) in March of 2008.

Since we've been here, (about four years now), we have built the workshop (with accompanying bedrooms), two lovely "cabins," but not the house. We knew from the beginning that this project would require lots of work... but the kind of work we both love... lots of gardening, cooking, entertaining and the like. We still love all those things.

309

We came here with the commitment to stay until we decided to either stay some more, or leave and do something else. I think we all have "blind sides"... things that we are either in denial about, or just don't give enough attention to. And so it's come to pass that it's not a question of "if" but rather of "when" as we will have family responsibilities in the states that require us to be there. Though we are in no hurry whatsoever to leave, and will be enormously sad to do so, we have made the decision to prepare ourselves ahead of time for the inevitable.

This is not to say that we won't leave the U.S. again. To the contrary, we are both bitten fairly severely by the travel bug, and always have been. There are family obligations to address, and my guess is that we will have more adventures outside of the U.S. when those are met.

I have read, and agree with Arden's perception that some people move here and don't like it for one reason or another. Others come here as an adventure, without thinking that Costa Rica is their final destination, and continue with their lives in other places. We are of the latter group. We have been totally enriched by our time and experience here, and haven't regretted for a moment, the decision to come here. But, there are other places in the world to visit, explore and be enriched by. We previewed New Zealand not long ago... (though it is very difficult, if not impossible to acquire residency there.) Spain is high on our list, as is Italy, to spend some time, perhaps have a project, and get to know their cultures. For some, Costa Rica is the end-all of all end-alls. To us it has been a grand adventure, but not the last stop on the path.

Index

A Broad in Costa Rica, 237, 294
Ackley, Tom, 307
Altitude. *See* Elevation
Appliances, 30, 139
Arenal, 57, 99

Blogs, 237
Boomers in Costa Rica tour, 247
Boxes, 192, 194, 198
Boyce, Marcia, 298

Cabinas, 35, 131
CAJA (medical insurance), 283
Carga Tica, 226
Choose Costa Rica for
    Retirement, John Howells,
    241
Container, cost, 137, 222, 279
Container, loading, 87, 100, 104,
    105, 111, 200
Container, sharing, 224
Container, size, 176
Coolers, 155
Cost of living, 34, 59, 73, 79,
    81, 267, 271
Crafting, 166
Crocodiles, 57
Culture shock, 66, 71
Customer service (lack thereof),
    64

Debit card, problem with, 56
Dehumidifying, 169
Dreaming of Costa Rica, 12
Driving, 57

Earnng a living, 286
Electronics, 169, 195
Elevation, 255, 260

Fifty to Life, 294

Financing the move, 83, 280,
    291
Fireplace, 162
Furniture, 30, 137, 157, 196,
    197
Furniture, outdoor, 151

Gallo pinto, 25, 26, 33
Gardening, 37, 38, 149
Golfito, 140
Grecia, 18, 22, 29
Gringo, use of term, 5
Gulf of Nicoya, 33, 45

Heredia, 22, 254

Inventory, 182, 211
Isolation, 70, 262

Kitchenware, 152, 154
Know yourself, 64, 289

La Posada, 30
Ladders, 148
Las Terrazas B&B, 18
LCL (Less than Container
    Load), 224, 226
Living Abroad in Costa Rica,
    Erin Van Rheenen, 241
Lizano, 25
Lundquist, George, 21, 28,
    248

Mattresses, 158, 199
Medical costs, 282, 284
Mi Choza (Mi Chosa), 31
Missing items, 217
Mosquitoes, 24
Moving back, 16, 17, 68, 74,
    290, 293

New Golden Door, Christopher Howard, 242
Notice (giving, at work). *See* Telling people:Work

O'Boyle, Sally, 237, 294
Orosi, 22, 44
Orozco, Adrian, 132
Owens, Jeanetta, 18

Pacific Ocean, 33, 57
Packing, 192
Pets, traveling with, 85, 117, 130
Pico Blanco, 41
Plastic tubs, 150, 193
Plaza Occidente, 36
Pops ice cream, 31
Puriscal, 22, 39

Ramp (for loading), 203
Reasons (for moving), 59, 73, 277
Rent before you buy, 54, 69, 81, 290
Retire on Social Security tour, 21, 72, 245
Rice, Martin, 16

San Jose, 22, 44, 253
San Ramon, 30, 34, 35, 45, 254
Sarchi, 30, 137, 143
Single, being, 69, 303
Spanish, speaking, 61, 198, 261

Square-rigged ship sailing, 59
Storage, 215
Suicide shower, 39, 41
Suitcases (bringing stuff in), 114, 226, 280
Swimming pool, 162

Tarcoles River, 57
Telling people
Family, 91, 94
Friends, 95
Work, 15, 89
Third World status, 13
Tico Times, 239
Time zone, 24, 99
Tools, 147
Type A personality, 66

U-Haul, 194, 196
University of Costa Rica, 254

Vehicle, bringing, 204
Vehicles, bringing, 86, 108

Wall Street Journal, 3
Walmart, 27, 63
Weather, 9, 13, 250, 260, 262
Websites, 234, 235, 237, 239
Wilson, Barry, 42, 135, 175
Windy season, 10, 263
Wish list, 257, 264
Worth, Mae, 303
Wrong, doing everything, 53

Mainers in Costa Rica, the series
Upcoming Books

Thirty Days of Food (coming out next!)

How to adjust to cooking and eating in a foreign country, or helpful hints for happiness in the kitchen and at the dinner table. In Part One you'll read a general overview, the quest for "real food," some suggestions for kitchen gear, and some detail on specific ingredients (where to buy and what to smuggle in!); Part Two offers over 150 pages of recipes and cooking tips, along with a glimpse into daily life for a gringo family in Costa Rica.

On the Road in Costa Rica (due out in 2011)

Should you ship a car or buy one here? Are the roads really as bad as they say? What's it like to really drive here? Can you get by without a car? Read about our experiences with the ins and outs of cars, roads, and driving in Costa Rica and get a detailed look at shipping a car here.

You're Here, Now What?

Our continuing adventures as we move through our first few years in Costa Rica. Explore—as we did—the questions of renting, building, or buying, how to deal with the day-to-day practicalities of life such as mail, phone, banking, hiring household help, making friends, and celebrating holidays in a new land.

You're Spending *How Much* a Month?

Real stories of real people and how much it costs them to live in Costa Rica with sample of costs for all kinds of stuff that you'll likely need to spend money on. We'll look not only at our own expenses but also at others who live on quite a bit more *and* less than we do.

The Sandwich Generation: Bringing Your Parents (Or Your Kids) With You

For some folks, one of the only things keeping them in the states is their aging parents. What if you bring the 'rents with you? Here's an in-depth look at our own experiences of having my parents living (and dying) with us here in Costa Rica, plus insightful stories from other friends here who've done the same.

And what if it's not your parents but your kids? We also look at families who have moved here with school age children as well as some whose "kids" are fully grown and looking to Costa Rica not for a "some day retirement" but for real life, right now.

Living (and Dying) in Costa Rica, A Health and Medical Perspective

In depth look at our own medical experiences here (which are extensive) with additional stories and experiences from a wide range of friends. Using the CAJA vs. the private system—most folks (us included) use both, so how do the two fit together. Health insurance, doctors, drugs, supplements, surgery, hospitalization, dental, cosmetic procedures... all are covered, right up through the final medical (and cultural) experience of dying in Costa Rica.

Your New Home in Costa Rica, Some Lessons Learned

When you move to Costa Rica, you've got several choices for housing—rent, buy land and build, or buy an existing house with or without lots of remodeling to do. We've "been there, done that" for most all of those options and have friends to fill in the blanks for whatever we haven't done. You don't have to reinvent the wheel—learn from those who have already been nearly run over by that same wheel!

www.mainersincostarica.com